The Curious Person's Guide to
Fighting Fake News

DAVID G. MCAFEE

Pitchstone Publishing
Durham, North Carolina

Pitchstone Publishing
Durham, North Carolina
www.pitchstonepublishing.com

10 9 8 7 6 5 4 3 2 1

Library of Congress Cataloging-in-Publication Data

Names: McAfee, David G., author.
Title: The curious person's guide to fighting fake news / David G. McAfee.
Description: Durham : Pitchstone Publishing, 2020. | Includes
  bibliographical references. | Summary: "Journalist David G. McAfee
  documents the myriad definitions of "fake news" and its various
  incarnations throughout history, from ideologically motivated
  disinformation operations to commercially motivated misinformation
  campaigns, and he presents a number of practical and actionable
  suggestions for combating it"— Provided by publisher.
Identifiers: LCCN 2020021706 (print) | LCCN 2020021707 (ebook) | ISBN
  9781634312066 (paperback) | ISBN 9781634312073 (ebook)
Subjects: LCSH: Fake news—United States. | Media literacy—United States.
Classification: LCC PN4888.F35 M33 2020 (print) | LCC PN4888.F35 (ebook)
  | DDC 070.4—dc23
LC record available at https://lccn.loc.gov/2020021706
LC ebook record available at https://lccn.loc.gov/2020021707

The Curious Person's Guide to *Fighting Fake News*

"As we express our gratitude, we must never forget that the highest appreciation is not to utter words, but to live by them."

—John F. Kennedy, U.S. president

Contents

Acknowledgments

This book is dedicated to Rae, my wife, editor, and best friend for all time, and to my amazing new friends, Heather Hernandez and James F. Wall Jr., who have helped make this book possible by continually supporting my work. Heather advocates for better lives through continuing education, and she's passionate about social justice, rights for immigrants, and celebrating diversity. James, who has a background in biological sciences, values scientific advancement, including fighting climate change and promoting the use of life-saving vaccines. Both James and Heather are dedicated opponents of dangerous pseudoscience.

Introduction: Can Journalism Really Accomplish Anything?

"I still believe that if your aim is to change the world, journalism is a more immediate short-term weapon."

—Sir Tom Stoppard, playwright

It's not very often that a simple conversation completely changes your mindset or truly inspires you. When that happens to me, I like to take advantage of it.

I had one such conversation while I was planning to write this book, and it caused me to change my direction for the work entirely. I was initially looking at the "fake news" problem as though it was caused by the *readers*, with journalists being innocent bystanders. After all, if there's no market for it, you can disincentivize fake news and at least reduce the volume of it greatly. There's certainly some truth to this perspective, but nobody needs a book by a journalist talking down to everyone who doesn't respect the profession. Not just because it's not palatable, but also because it doesn't paint an accurate portrait of reality.

Instead, the problem, and its origins, are much more complex than that. It took a younger but extremely mature individual calling me out on the subject of journalism and fake news to see that. I now understand that we are all culpable in the current fake news pandemic, and that we can all do our parts to help fix it. I also see that journalism itself has its own flaws, and that it must evolve along with every other industry as our technology changes and understanding of the world improves.

So, a simple conversation with a kid sparked a change that would ultimately set these pages ablaze. The book you're reading went from a lecture by a reporter to everyone else, to a discussion about where we can go in this world if we actually work together to fight the misinformation mayhem . . . all because of a dialogue. Here's how that conversation went:

In April 2017, I was approached by a young man as I was signing books at the Los Angeles Times Festival of Books at the University of Southern California (USC). He appeared to be about 12 years old, and he was definitely confrontational, but he was also extremely well spoken and obviously incredibly intelligent. He started off by criticizing journalism and the media, saying modern-day news reports only reinforce what we already believe, which is often the case, unfortunately. He also made the very correct point that many "news" agencies care more about clicks and controversy than they do about spreading good information, which has been a problem for as long as I can remember.

He and I had a spirited conversation in which I explained to him my position that *good journalism* does the opposite of what he was saying. True investigative reporting is all about the *truth*, and passing on quality information to those who may not have it or be able to obtain it for themselves. It takes your preconceived notions and *dismantles* them using facts, logic, and evidence. It's not an easy process, I said, but when reporters do good work, they can challenge what *they* already believed—as well as the beliefs of readers.

I told him that he's right to point out the shortage of proper journalism in modern media. In fact, I agreed with him that irresponsible reporting is perhaps at an all-time high, and that it was indeed a true crisis. But despite that, quality journalism still exists, and we should seek it out and encourage it at all costs. All other options ensure that *real news* is crushed under the weight of bullshit, and there's no telling where that could lead.

Getting rid of biases and challenging your own bad thinking is a key to good journalism, and it's also rarely seen in today's media, I added. But if we write off journalism entirely, and accept that the landscape will forever be littered with so-called fake news that distracts from the facts, we will never be able to reap the rewards of intelligent reporting. Specifically, we won't be able to solve some of the big problems that *real* journalists—who investigate for the sake of finding the truth—can.

"The good journalism needs to be able to happen, and when people write off journalism in general, saying it can't solve anything, it impedes that. It makes people less likely to try," I told him.

The young man said he appreciated my points, and admitted that his "own biases" may have been informing his views. He noted that he's "frustrated" as a "kid living in the current era" who hasn't really *seen* much great journalism.

I said I understood his concerns, and that I actually felt the same way much of the time, and we started to discuss the future of journalism. But I told him that it is important to look at the past as well. If we look at the history of the United States, and even the world, we can find many major developments that only came through investigative writing. I told him that horrible actions, put forth by governments and individuals alike, have been exposed thanks to people who ask good questions. And that's most of what journalism *really* is: asking good questions and fact-checking the answers.

Take Nellie Bly, for instance. She was one of the first American investigative journalists, and she went undercover to expose how mentally ill people were being abused at the New York City Lunatic Asylum (Markel, 2018). Bly, whose real name was Elizabeth Cochrane Seaman, changed how we look at mental health institutions and brought real and lasting positive changes to the industry. Journalists also helped reveal corruption within President Richard Nixon's administration during the height of the infamous Watergate scandal (Feldstein, 2016), exposed atrocities surrounding the Vietnam war, and much, much more.

Unfortunately, I explained, many people in today's society don't *care* about the truth. They don't even want facts. They are more interested in what makes them feel good, or what makes them feel justified in their prior behaviors. In essence, there are a lot of *consumers* who crave the current clickbait culture. But there are still some people—like me and like this young boy—who *do* care about what's really happening.

He made another good point about the "sheer volume" of news, including true and false reports alike, which he said makes it hard to parse through and discover what's valuable to you. The variety of perspectives, with everyone skewing "truth" to their preferred directions, makes things seem "futile," he said.

And he was right. A big part of the problem is that fake news has become completely unavoidable; we see intentionally false or misleading information basically everywhere.

But a diversity of opinions is the reality, and it's not always bad . . . as long as people can separate those perspectives from facts.

I told the kid that the problem isn't necessarily a plethora of perspectives—that should actually be a good thing. We have to look deeper. To me, I said, it seems like the real issue is *confirma-*

tion bias and how humans are ruled by it. We tend to look at the "news" sources that cater to our preexisting beliefs, and rarely challenge our thinking or what we already accept to be true. Then comes the secondary concern, which is the abundance of "news" sites spewing nonsense all over the world. That wouldn't be all that bad if humans weren't predisposed to confirmation bias, but since we are, we often see good journalism drowned out by misinformation.

"This isn't a lesson in futility. It's a lesson that teaches us we have to do better," I told him. "We have to improve our journalistic standards. We have to fight against fake news, against propaganda, and against lies in the media."

The boy agreed, and said he had a lot to think about. We went our separate ways, but that conversation never *really* left my mind. In fact, I thought about it a lot going forward.

I thought about how, while part of the blame can and should be placed on bad journalism and clickbait culture, the antijournalism stance can also be one based on privilege. This young man grew up in a world that was made a better place because of journalism, and he's now able to take that situation for granted. In a way, you could say that journalism's success has also led to its potential downfall.

I also thought about how *other* people view this subject. As it turns out, this young man isn't the only one who doubts journalism's viability. According to media theorist Douglas Rushkoff, college students frequently play down the importance of media. "College students often ask me why anyone should pay for professional journalism when there are plenty of people out there, like themselves, willing to write blogs for free?" he writes in Present Shock: When Everything Happens Now. "One answer is that government and corporations are investing millions of dollars into their professional communications campaigns. We deserve at least a few professionals working full-time to evaluate all this messaging and doing so with some level of expertise in ascertaining the truth."

Rushkoff added that young people are "not alone in their skepticism about the value of professional journalism," pointing to a 2010 Gallup Poll that showed Americans at a record low for confidence in newspapers and television news.

My talk with this kid certainly represented a larger pattern of generational divides on this issue. And it made me think about how future generations will view journalism, and about whether or not that perception can be salvaged. It made me want to tell the world about the *good* that investigative writing can do—how it can change lives and impact the world. It made me want to write this book. So, that's what I did.

1 The Rise of Fake News

"The media's so central to our lives that we believe what we see onscreen is real. In fact, it's more real than reality: emotions are heightened, drama sharpened, issues simplified."

—Steve Shahbazian, author

References to "fake news" are not just common but extremely widespread. They can be found *everywhere*, from the White House on down. Archival searches reveal President Donald Trump used the term "fake news" about 150 times on Twitter alone between January 1, 2017 and January 1, 2018, a period of just one year.[1] As of November 30, 2019, he had tweeted the words "fake news" 596 times.[2]

It's not just him, though. While President Trump has said that he created the term himself, that itself may be fake news. The world's largest legal association—the American Bar Associ-

---

1. My own Twitter analysis.
2. Trump Twitter Archive, www.trumptwitterarchive.com/archive.

ation—contradicts Trump's invention claim. The exact phrase has been used since at least 1993, according to the association, which mentioned the left-leaning Center for Democracy & Technology's PR Watch and its "Stop Fake News!" campaign (Kirtley, n.d.). It was also reportedly used beginning in the fall of 2014, before Trump's first public usage, by BuzzFeed News media editor Craig Silverman (Beaujon, 2019). Even Hillary Clinton, Trump's rival in the 2016 election, used "fake news" before Trump did, according to the BBC (Wendling, 2018). Indeed, the term "fake news" has seen its share of usage over the years. And the idea behind it has been around much longer than any of those examples.

President Trump may not have come up with the designation, but he did become a popularizer of it, ultimately helping it take over the whole world. "Fake news" has been uttered by Democratic presidential candidates, such as Tulsi Gabbard, D–Hawaii (Beavers, 2019), as well as by foreign leaders, and the term has been invoked in nearly every political and social context imaginable.

Although we've all heard a lot about "fake news" in recent years, you probably don't have a solid definition in mind. So, before explaining exactly how to fight it, it might help to *define* the term itself, which is often used to refer to just about anything that isn't favorable to an individual, and to give some historical context on the issue. To start, let's turn to Collins Dictionary, which named "fake news" one of its words of the year in 2017. Collins defines it as *"false, often sensational, information disseminated under the guise of news reporting"* (Singh, 2017).

That's a pretty good definition, and here are some others:

Fake News [feyk nooz]
noun phrase

1. False stories that appear to be news, spread on the internet

or using other media, usually created to influence political views or as a joke. (Cambridge University Press, n.d.)

2. False news stories, often of a sensational nature, created to be widely shared or distributed for the purpose of generating revenue, or promoting or discrediting a public figure, political movement, company, etc. (Dictionary.com, n.d.)

   Example sentence: I saw a fake news story falsely claiming Oprah died, so I posted an article from Snopes in the comments.

These are the definitions from various dictionaries, but the fact is people have been dealing with similar issues since long before the term "fake news" was coined, and people still can't agree on what constitutes fake news items. What some people might refer to as fake news, I'd be just as comfortable calling "bullshit." And there are several other synonyms, too.

Some definitions further fail to mention or specify one key aspect of fake news: it often takes on the outward appearance of a piece of traditional journalism, but without the standard controls applied to reporters. Because fake news is so convincing and often looks like real news to the untrained eye, reading a piece of fake news triggers the same feelings we get every time we learn something new. We can also get the same aha moment—even if the sudden realization is based on faulty information. And that moment, as well as the superiority one can feel from learning something they think others don't know, is part of why fake news and conspiracy theories are addictive (as I will discuss later).

Despite the lack of a single, informative definition, "fake news" has become a popular phrase in recent years. Still, the issues that underly the accusation are much deeper and older.

History of Misinformation and Propaganda

Misinformation (Misinformation, n.d.), which is defined as false information intentionally propagated to deceive, and *disinformation*, usually used to refer to inaccurate or skewed reports coming from a government organization (Disinformation, n.d.), have a long history of affecting our society. The only real difference now is that their platforms are of an unprecedented size.

Even though the rise of the internet has greatly increased the range of fake news, and the rate of its spread, it wasn't the *first* innovation to shake things up in that way. While misinformation has probably existed for as long as communication itself, it got a significant boost thanks to Johannes Gutenberg. I'm talking, of course, about the printing press. Jonathan Grudin, a principal design researcher at Microsoft, put it this way:

> We were in this position before, when the printing presses broke the existing system for information management. A new system emerged and I believe we have the motivation and capability to do it again.

It was the Gutenberg press that ultimately gave way to what is recognized as the first major large-scale hoax, also known as the 1835 "Great Moon Hoax," published in the *New York Sun*. The series of articles claimed a variety of life had been discovered on the moon, and it included illustrations of anthropomorphized bat-creatures and goat-bearded unicorns, according to the International Center for Journalists (Posetti & Matthews, 2018).

From there on, hoaxes and misinformation were pretty common in various forms of media but remained flat in terms of general volume. The next massive paradigm shift for fake news came with yet another new medium: radio. With radio's rising popularity came another major fake news event, even if those involved didn't intend it to be so. That event was Orson Welles's 1938 performance of an adaptation of *The War of the Worlds* by H.G. Wells, a story from the late 1800s describing a conflict between humans and alien visitors. Although Welles always maintained he never *intended* to deceive people to the extent he did, the broadcast did cause some panic from people who misinterpreted what was happening as real, and thought Earth was under attack by extraterrestrials (Schwartz, 2015).

It wasn't long after Welles catapulted to fame with his dramatic retelling mistaken for a news report that the next big fake news event took place. This time, it was in the form of political propaganda. During World War II, the Nazi regime created what is arguably considered one of the most notorious disinformation campaigns of all time. This included spreading lies, attacking reporters, and burning books as part of the dictatorship's plot to control all forms of media, according to the *Holocaust Encyclopedia* (United States Holocaust Memorial Museum, n.d.). This attempt to take over the media in Germany included the denigration of existing news platforms, using the term *"Lügenpresse"* (or lying press) as a means to cast doubt on credible news reports. (I will cover this more in chapter 4.)

Fake news continued to grow in presence as TV's popularity rose, and several high-profile pieces of misinformation *and* disinformation took root in our culture. Things only got worse with the spread of the internet, which further added an instant-gratification effect to the crisis of harmful fake news.

Modern Misinformation

It's clear that demeaning the media is a time-honored tradition, so what's new? Well, since the creation of the internet and technology that has led to its spread to nearly every community in the world, information is becoming more accessible for almost everyone. On one hand, that has meant the cumulative human knowledge is at our fingertips in an instant, creating the potential for doing great things.

That being said, as I've written before, the Age of Information also means the Age of *Disinformation*. That same technology that allows us to learn anything in an instant is what allows scammers to perpetuate massive frauds from anywhere in the world. Similarly, the modern landscape has allowed fake news—including life-endangering misinformation—to proliferate faster and reach more minds than ever. Abhijit Naskar, author of *The Constitution of the United Peoples of Earth*, has eloquently put it this way:

> Before the invention of printing press, the problem was, lack of information, and now due to the rise of social media, it is too much information—the former leads to mental starvation and the latter to mental obesity.

This rapid spread of content on social media also leads people to frequently see the same fake news items over and over again, which cements the untrue notions in their heads, regardless of the veracity or lack thereof. One study from 2018 revealed that fake news, defined as "entirely fabricated and often partisan content that is presented as factual," is more believable when it's repeated—even if it is debunked by fact-checkers (Pennycock, Cannon, & Rand, 2018):

> These results suggest that social media platforms help to incubate belief in blatantly false news stories, and that tagging such stories as disputed is not an effective solution to this problem.

It would be one thing if fake news simply gained the same technological advantage as news in general, proliferating at higher rates year after year but keeping pace with its counterpart that *doesn't* rely on faulty information. Unfortunately, it's not that simple. Because of how our brains work, it turns out that fake news is likely edging out the truth. In other words, "Lies spread faster than the truth," according to a study that analyzed the issue (Vosoughi, Roy, & Aral, 2018):

> Falsehood diffused significantly farther, faster, deeper, and more broadly than the truth in all categories of information, and the effects were more pronounced for false political news than for false news about terrorism, natural disasters, science, urban legends, or financial information. We found that false news was more novel than true news, which suggests that people were more likely to share novel information.

None of that even touches on another major factor in today's world of information processing: bots. In past generations, creating hysteria through a whisper campaign would have meant employing thousands of individual paid protesters. Then you'd have to rely on them to do the job (in this case, spreading dangerous rumors). Today, you pay a much smaller fee to employ a bot service that you *know* will spread the material you want to get out there. This isn't just a theory; this is happening right now.

Social media bots play a "key role" in the spread of fake news, which some say has the potential to influence elections, and weening away from that technology may actually help the problem, according to a 2018 study (Shao, et al., 2018):

> We find evidence that social bots played a disproportionate role in amplifying low-credibility content. Accounts that actively spread articles from low-credibility sources are significantly more likely to be bots. Automated accounts are partic-

ularly active in amplifying content in the very early spreading moments, before an article goes viral. Bots also target users with many followers through replies and mentions. Humans are vulnerable to this manipulation, retweeting bots who post links to low-credibility content. Successful low-credibility sources are heavily supported by social bots. These results suggest that curbing social bots may be an effective strategy for mitigating the spread of online misinformation.

With the spread of fake news at an all-time high due to a combination of factors, including technology like bots but also because of heightened political partisanship, it makes sense that there would be a pushback against those who spread bad information. What you might not think about, though, is the casualty of that: the legitimate media.

Reporters have become collateral damage in a war between humanity and those who provide misinformation. In some cases, they've become cannon fodder used by bad actors who hope to disguise what they're doing and cast the spotlight on anyone else. People (or organizations or countries) like this want you to conflate "news" and "fake news" so that their nonsense carries as much weight as thoroughly researched, vetted information provided by real news groups.

While this makes sense from the logical and self-preservation perspectives, it's crucial that we not allow that to happen and instead help journalism regain its former glory. I don't say this as a journalist, but as someone who lives in society and has seen firsthand the important role such work has played. Maybe it would help for journalism to get back to its roots in exposing corruption.

New technologies and bots are part of how people can access fake news from anywhere in the world at any time of the day, and that is part of what has made it *addictive*.

2 We're All Addicted to Fake News

"[S]pread, rather than fakeness, is the birthmark of these contents that should be called 'viral news' or possibly 'junk news' for, just as junk food, they are consumed because they are addictive, not because they are appreciated."

—Tommaso Venturini, media researcher

We all know *someone* who is addicted to fake news or other forms of false information spread online or in other popular media. It could be an aunt who watches *only* Fox News, or a brother who spends all his time viewing conspiracy theory videos on YouTube, or—if you can't think of anyone in your life who fits this description—it could be *you*. In fact, I intend to show you that we are *all* addicted to fake news . . . or at least we are all predisposed to believing in it. So, how do we fix a problem that's based on the very nature of who we are as human beings? That's the entire purpose of this book.

When I say everyone is addicted to fake news, I mean just that: we all have pretty much the same brain structure, and as a result we are all encouraged to consume and believe false information *on a chemical level*. To be more specific, we get pleasure from reading stories that confirm our beliefs—similar to the positive feelings all addicts get when they engage in the behavior to which they're addicted—and displeasure from those that challenge them. That means that, regardless of the veracity of the underlying claims, our brains reward us for reading those opinions with which we already agree. This creates a *natural echo-chamber* in which we are compelled to take in what makes us feel good over what's demonstrably true. Two of the phenomena that ensure this will happen are *selective exposure* and *cognitive dissonance*, which can work together to change how people intake essentially all information. Research has shown these effects on news viewers are quite significant. In one study on selective exposure in 1991, the authors found that "consonance and dissonance between messages and readers' predispositions have a statistically significant but rather limited impact on exposure" (Donsbach, 1991):

> [T]he findings seem to indicate that newspaper readers have a slight but statistically significant tendency to expose themselves to information which is supportive of their already existing opinions about politicians in the news. This general pattern is conditional, however, on a number of interacting variables.

Several years after that breakthrough paper, a follow-up study found that a "substantial proportion of the public" consumes "media sharing their political predispositions" (Stroud, 2008):

> Of the media types evaluated in this study, 64 percent of conservative Republicans consume at least one conservative

media outlet compared to 26 percent of liberal Democrats. In contrast, 43 percent of conservative Republicans consume at least one liberal outlet while 76 percent of liberal Democrats consume at least one liberal outlet. These striking percentages document the extent of partisan selective exposure in the contemporary media environment.

This study investigates whether people's political predispositions motivate their media selections. The evidence clearly suggests that this is the case. Both in the cross-sectional and panel analyses, people's political predispositions predict their selection of political talk radio, cable news, and Internet websites. Even with a control for the partisanship make-up of their congressional district, people's political beliefs are related to the newspapers they read.

You might be thinking it's obvious that people would consume material that fits in with their side of the political spectrum, and that may be true, but it definitely isn't *good*. Part of being intellectually honest is exposing ourselves to conflicting ideas, and learning from them. If we are right, that process makes our arguments stronger. If we are wrong, it gives us a chance to *become right* by learning from other perspectives. If we don't look at disagreeable content, we miss out on an opportunity to learn more *and* risk getting stuck in a cycle of comfortable-yet-wrong thinking.

What's the Problem?

Cognitive dissonance, the uncomfortable feeling humans get when we hold contradicting viewpoints, is one of the reasons people tend to avoid ideas that go against their own. While many people discount the power of cognitive dissonance, it is an extremely strong motivator. The phenomenon can also be measured scientifically, according to researchers (Izuma, n.d.):

> What is the neural explanation for this common type of psychological stress? Thanks to advances in imaging methods, especially functional MRI, researchers have recently identified key brain regions linked to cognitive dissonance. The area implicated most consistently is the posterior part of the medial frontal cortex (pMFC), known to play an important role in avoiding aversive outcomes, a powerful built-in survival instinct. In fMRI studies, when subjects lie to a peer despite knowing that lying is wrong—a task that puts their actions and beliefs in conflict—the pMFC lights up.
>
> Recently my colleagues and I demonstrated a causal link between pMFC activity and the attitude change required to reduce dissonance. We induced cognitive dissonance in 52 participants by having them rate two wallpapers. When asked to evaluate their choices on a second viewing, some participants realized that they had actually rejected their preferred wallpaper, whereas others had initially chosen their least favorite option. We found that by temporarily decreasing activity in the pMFC using a technique called transcranial magnetic stimulation (TMS), we could also diminish their attitude changes and their desire to create consistency.

Keise Izuma, who lectures on social cognitive neuroscience, further noted that cognitive dissonance engages the insula and dorsolateral prefrontal cortex (DLPFC). The researcher also explained the lesser-known *positive aspects* of the feeling, which most people unfortunately spend their entire lives trying to escape:

> Although people may think cognitive dissonance is a bad thing, it actually helps to keep us mentally healthy and happy.

It may make us feel satisfied with our choices—or at least lets us justify them—especially when they cannot be easily reversed. Resolving dissonance may help prevent us from making bad choices or motivate us to make good ones. This desire to be at peace with our decisions might be just the thing to inspire us to go for that run after all.

Cognitive dissonance can be a beneficial learning tool, as well as something that aids in our survival, if we can utilize it properly. More often than not, however, we run from this feeling. And as a result, we usually end up selectively choosing books, videos, and websites that support our existing opinions. That pattern then reinforces itself and we don't learn anything.

People can be addicted to just about anything that gives them pleasure, including drugs, alcohol, and the internet. Even gambling, shopping, and sex can "highjack" the brain, according to Harvard's medical school newsletter (Harvard Medical School, 2011):

> The brain registers all pleasures in the same way, whether they originate with a psychoactive drug, a monetary reward, a sexual encounter, or a satisfying meal. In the brain, pleasure has a distinct signature: the release of the neurotransmitter dopamine in the nucleus accumbens, a cluster of nerve cells lying underneath the cerebral cortex. Dopamine release in the nucleus accumbens is so consistently tied with pleasure that neuroscientists refer to the region as the brain's pleasure center.
>
> Addictive drugs provide a shortcut to the brain's reward system by flooding the nucleus accumbens with dopamine. The hippocampus lays down memories of this rapid sense of satisfaction, and the amygdala creates a conditioned response to certain stimuli.

If pleasurable activities release dopamine in the brain, and we are *wired* to get bad feelings from taking in information with which we disagree, it makes sense that we would want to swim in an ocean of agreeable data. But that doesn't mean it's a *positive thing*.

To be clear, I'm not saying that reading news you agree with is as addictive as drugs like meth or crack. We have seen studies that show how technology and social media can be addictive themselves to a certain extent, and this is just the same principle extended. What I am saying, however, is that the trend toward exclusivity in news is understandable and completely natural. That makes it even more important to understand how it works, and how to fight back and potentially improve the situation that we find ourselves in.

Sunk-Cost Effect

A version of the *sunk-cost effect*, which describes the tendency for people to continue investing money in a failing project, could also come into play here. Studies have shown that cognitive dissonance plays a role in this sunk-cost phenomenon (Chung, 2018), but there are a lot of different factors. Although many people associate it with economic investments alone, the truth is that the same logic can be relevant when *anything* is invested: time, love, etc. In politics, people who are born into families with strong partisan beliefs often inherit those same ideals and then have to confront cognitive dissonance as they see where they're wrong over time. They have likely invested years in their faulty political paradigm, but the sunk-cost fallacy keeps them from acknowledging that. In order to compensate for the uncomfortable feelings, some people will choose to throw themselves deeper into the ideology and ignore anything that contradicts it. In 2018, an assistant professor of marketing at Carnegie

Mellon's Tepper School of Business actually found that the effect "is a much broader phenomenon than previously thought" (Olivola, 2018):

> The sunk-cost effect is a broader phenomenon than previously thought, which generalizes to interpersonal investment contexts. Across eight experiments representing a wide variety of scenarios adapted from the classic sunk-cost literature, I repeatedly observed a sunk-cost effect when the person incurring the cost was someone other than the decision maker. Moreover, this occurred even when that person would not observe whether the decision maker honored his or her sunk cost, suggesting that social desirability is not a key driver.

I spoke with the researcher, Chris Olivola, about how we see sunk-cost reasoning displayed in politics. He said diving deeper into a political party because you've already "invested" in it is one example, but that it "could also be a case of dissonance reduction." Olivola added:

> An example of the interpersonal sunk-cost fallacy in politics would be a politician (e.g., president or state governor) who continues investing in a failing policy project (e.g., building an expensive bridge that goes over budget, or continuing to send soldiers into a losing war) merely because his/her predecessor (i.e., the previous president or governor) had invested a lot of money on solders' lives on that project.

To sum up, even if people *want* to find reliable news (which is already an uncertainty considering current apathy levels), several factors within our own bodies and minds work against that. It's almost as if we are all addicted to news we *agree with*, whether or not it is true, and that makes us a prime target for *fake news*.

Our natural tendency to support our preconceived notions and isolate ourselves from conflicting information, combined with our innate desire to continue along a path to which we've already committed, is our undoing. It makes it easy to get caught in a cycle of faulty, one-sided reports, which is bad for any democracy.

Opposing Views

So, what if we made sure people were exposed to "the other side" as well? That would almost certainly work, wouldn't it? The truth is the answer isn't that simple. Both traditional media outlets and social media companies are already starting to explore methods of exposing people to alternative viewpoints as a mechanism to deal with the rampant fake news and hyperpartisan rhetoric. Take the *Guardian*, for instance, a left-leaning outlet that started a weekly "Burst Your Bubble" column that provides "conservative articles worth reading to expand your thinking."

Surprisingly, studies have shown this *could actually* make things worse. In one study, Republicans became *more conservative*[3] after being exposed to Twitter bots that retweeted prominent liberal figures (Bail, 2018). This happened because the nature of echo chambers is that those who exist in them are typically less likely to try to persuade the "other side," and therefore less likely to understand the opposition's arguments. So when these Twitter users were exposed to posts by high-profile people with contradictory views, they were seeing statements meant to pander to the base of their opposites. Republicans saw tweets geared toward the most liberal of Americans, and it just confirmed their worst fears and made them more

---

3. Democrats in the study also became slightly more liberal, but that data was statistically insignificant.

secure in their beliefs.

It turns out that the answer to hyperpartisanism, which itself causes fake news through the spread of overly biased/opinionated statements disguised as facts, can't be found through simple exposure to opposing views. Perhaps it takes exposing people to more centrist viewpoints first, or to comments that are specifically tailored to convince those with extreme political differences. It's also possible that we don't *know* the answer yet.

What we *do* know is that the circumstances in which we find ourselves were predicted by science-fiction writer Isaac Asimov, who once said there was a "cult of ignorance"[4] in the United States, as well as by Carl Sagan himself:

> The dumbing down of America is most evident in the slow decay of substantive content in the enormously influential media, the 30 second sound bites (now down to 10 seconds or less), lowest common denominator programming, credulous presentations on pseudoscience and superstition, but especially a kind of celebration of ignorance.

I don't know exactly how we all got hooked on fake news, but I can tell you how we can get out of the current predicament: we have to start valuing facts again. I'm a firm believer in the idea that the biggest problem we face—the most dangerous aspect of our modern society—isn't conservatism or liberalism. It isn't gun control or access to guns. It isn't any "hot-button issue." It is the glorification of ignorance. Not knowing something is fine, but too many people today are *proud* of not knowing and don't want to fix it.

---

4. "There is a cult of ignorance in the United States, and there always has been. The strain of anti-intellectualism has been a constant thread winding its way through our political and cultural life, nurtured by the false notion that democracy means that 'my ignorance is just as good as your knowledge.'" —Isaac Asimov

3 Fake News as a Defense Mechanism

"One of the most troubling things about the term 'fake news'
is that it has become a force field against
accusations you don't like."

—Kevin Young, poet

I spent much of my life hoping that people would start paying attention to misinformation and disinformation. When I first heard the words "fake news" used to describe nonsense being published online, I thought maybe that time had finally come. Unfortunately, I was wrong. The term may have started off as a way to describe faulty or misleading information tainted with extreme political bias, but today it is used by people across the political spectrum to write off facts that make them look bad.

The term "fake news" caught fire in 2016 and continued to gain momentum in 2017 and for several years after that, but it didn't serve its original purpose: to point out intentionally false and/or misleading information being propagated, most often online. Instead, in what seemed like no time at all, anything that anyone disagreed with was being called "fake news."

Even after this shift, I thought massive public awareness of fake news could possibly make people better understand intentional propaganda and disinformation, which would allow them to more easily seek out facts. But I quickly learned it's not enough to slap a catchy label on lies and faulty reporting; we have to figure out why it happens and stop the problem it at its source.

The term "fake news" itself is deeply flawed and shouldn't be used, according to Joy Mayer, the founder of Trusting News, which works with journalists to improve their perceptions among members of the public.

In a phone interview, Mayer said:

I actually hate the term "fake news." I wish we would stop using it. If it's fake, it's not news. And I think the problem is the fact that it's been sort of co-opted by people who are using it to apply to information they disagree with. It seems like just a very typical sort of slur to hurl at journalists, as opposed to information that has a take or a frame that doesn't match my worldview, which is very often how it is used now.

This perspective is echoed by the *Washington Post*'s media columnist, Margaret Sullivan, who argued that it is time to "retire" the term "fake news" entirely. She stated that, despite there being a solid definition of fake news (which she says is "deliberately constructed lies, in the form of news articles, meant to mislead the public"), the term is completely beyond salvation because of its application toward anything with which a person happens to disagree (Sullivan, 2017):

But though the term hasn't been around long, its meaning already is lost. Faster than you could say 'Pizzagate,' the label

has been co-opted to mean any number of completely different things: Liberal claptrap. Or opinion from left-of-center.
Or simply anything in the realm of news that the observer
doesn't like to hear.

. . . .

Instead, call a lie a lie. Call a hoax a hoax. Call a conspiracy
theory by its rightful name. After all, 'fake news' is an impre-
cise expression to begin with.

Famous fact-checking site Snopes has used similar arguments for its decision not to use the term "fake news." Snopes
engagement editor Bond Huberman, who said the site favors
"junk news" to "emphasize the distinction between misinformation and content created purposely to deceive," writes the
following (Huberman, 2019):

> At Snopes we strive to contribute information to public dis-
> course, not subtract from it. If "fake news" can no longer
> reliably signal whether a piece of reporting is trustworthy,
> and instead behaves like a rhetorical middle finger, it doesn't
> have a place in our work.

I completely agree with this assessment from Sullivan, Huberman, and other experts. There is no shortage of times in
which "fake news" has been applied to mean whatever the
speaker wants it to mean, so much so that using it is no longer
effective. In many cases, this means it is used as a scapegoat to
avoid all liability for someone's actions.

I can think of no better example of this than the case of the
late Dan Johnson, a Republican Kentucky state representative
and pastor who also claimed to be a White House chaplain,
a United Nations ambassador, and a first responder on 9/11.
The last three of those are completely unconfirmed and could

be described by some people as "fake news."

Johnson found himself on the wrong end of some quality journalism in 2017, when the nonpartisan Kentucky Center for Investigative Reporting put out a multipart report showing not only that his biography was full of lies, but also that he was accused of sexually assaulting a young girl who was friends with his daughter (Dunlop & Ryan, 2017).

According to the report:

> Long ago, Johnson fashioned an identity as a modern-day American patriot. Pro-gun, pro-God, pro-life. He talked in 2013 about making America great again. He lamented the lack of God in everyone's lives. He wept over the country's future.
>
> But behind this persona—cultivated, built up and fine-tuned over decades—is a web of lies and deception. A mysterious fire. Attempted arson and false testimony. Alleged molestation in his church.
>
> In Johnson's wake lies a trail of police records and court files, shattered lives and a flagrant disregard for truth.

That in-depth report, based on a seven-month investigation involving countless interviews and "several thousand pages of public documents," brought a spotlight to Johnson that caused his entire house of cards to come crashing down.

It also led to something no one expected: Johnson, who called himself "the Pope" and frequently posted racist and anti-Islamic comments on social media, took his own life. He reportedly drove onto a bridge before shooting himself in front of his car. His body was found on the bank of a river, according to local reports (WDRB, 2017).

Just before Johnson killed himself, he posted a cryptic rant on Facebook in which he denied the allegations, blaming everything from "fake news" to post-traumatic stress disorder to "the Devil himself."

> The accusations from NPR are false GOD and only GOD knows the truth, nothing is the way they make it out to be. AMERICA will not survive this type of judge and jury fake news . Conservatives take a stand. I LOVE GOD and I LOVE MY WIFE, who is the best WIFE in the world,My Love Forever ! My Mom and Dad my FAMILY and all five of my kids and Nine grandchildren two in tummies and many more to come each of you or a total gift from GOD stay strong, REBECCA needs YOU . 9-11-2001 NYC/WTC, PTSD 24/7 16 years is a sickness that will take my life, I cannot handle it any longer. IT Has Won This Life . BUT HEAVEN IS MY HOME. "PLEASE LISTEN CLOSELY, Only Three things I ask of you to do,if you love me is (1) blame no person,Satan is the accuser, so blame the Devil himself. (2) Forgive and Love everyone especially yourself .(3) most importantly LOVE GOD. P.S. I LOVE MY FRIENDS YOU ARE FAMILY ! GOD LOVES ALL PEOPLE NO MATTER WHAT !⁵

There was a police investigation launched over Johnson's alleged molestation of this young girl, and he already had a pretty extensive criminal record (and was linked to multiple arsons). His story is a complicated one that likely should have ended in some serious prison time. I worry that he may now be seen as a martyr by his faithful followers who will blame legitimate journalists instead of accepting the truth.

In fact, almost immediately after his suicide, people who aligned ideologically with Johnson began to believe his letter

---

5. I chose to include all the author's typos as to retain the authenticity of the original message.

and blame the media, as opposed to the man who was credibly accused of sexually abusing an underage girl. The fact is, though, that it was not the media's fault that Johnson decided not to face the consequences of his illegal actions. The reporting, judging by the extent of the evidence, was solid. It was verified by dozens of people who knew Johnson throughout his life. Maybe Johnson's guilt finally caught up with him. Maybe he didn't want to face a future in which he was known for his lies instead of the myth he had crafted, all while sitting in a jail cell. We will never know exactly what led him to make that decision. What we do know, however, is that the media doesn't deserve the blame, and the report certainly wasn't fake news.

So, it is clear that "fake news" is used to refer to just about anything that an individual doesn't like, and I personally would love to do away with it. That being said, one study found that such a change away from the phrase fake news "won't happen easily" because consumers use the term for their own purposes (Nielsen & Graves, n.d.):

> While it is true that the term "fake news" is frequently used instrumentally for political advantage—a fact that ordinary people often recognize—it has also become part of the vernacular that helps people express their frustration with the media environment, because it resonates with their experience of coming across many different kinds of misinformation, especially online, and because it is used actively by critics of both news media and platforms.

The study further states that the fake news problem "is only in part about fabricated news reports" and that it also "reflects a deeper discontent with many public sources of information."

"It is clear that for ordinary news users, as indeed for journalists, politicians, and researchers, the word is not neatly divided into truth and falsehood," it says.

There are many reasons one might be drawn to a vague and controversial term like "fake news," and new research indicates fear may be a key component of that formula.

Role of Fear

Ironically, the people who cry "FAKE NEWS!" at every media report that challenges their thinking are the same people who continually *fall for* false reports. This isn't always because they are dumb, however. It's partly because we are all predisposed to believing in narratives that support what we already think is true, which I discussed earlier in this book, and partly because of an enhanced hazard detection in humans.

For example, after the 2016 election, we saw reports about conservatives being convinced more than liberals by fake news enterprises. According to multiple studies, it isn't that Republicans are more *stupid* or *gullible* than their liberal counterparts; it's because people who fall on the right side of the political spectrum tend to be more attuned to *all* threats—even imagined ones (Khazan, 2017). That means that, in this particular instance at least, fake news is allowed to propagate largely because of a simple *predisposition* toward rapid fear responses. And here's the kicker: those same fear responses exist because evolution favors them. It turns out "survival of the fittest" often means "survival of the safest," and taking perceived threats seriously is likely to keep you out of harm's way.

Another potential reason to use "fake news" as a defense mechanism is even simpler than the fear hypothesis: an inability to admit wrongness. This, too, is completely natural. It is normal for humans to *want* to be right, and to react poorly when proven wrong. These days, this can come out in the form of "fake news" accusations.

Indoctrination within families is a strong bond to break, and the one created by professional liars and deceivers is no different. In fact, even if we come up with a bad idea all on our own, it's hard to make that necessary revelation that we might be wrong. As the authors of *Mistakes Were Made (But Not by Me)* explain, this form of "self-justification" is not the same as "lying or making excuses" (Tavris, 2009):

> Obviously, people will lie or invent fanciful stories to duck the fury of a lover, parent, or employer; to keep from being sued or sent to prison; to avoid losing face; to avoid losing a job; to stay in power. But there is a big difference between what a guilty man says to the public to convince them of something he knows is untrue ("I did not have sex with that woman"; "I am not a crook"), and the process of persuading himself that he did a good thing. In the former situation, he is lying and knows he is lying to save his own skin. In the latter, he is lying to himself. That is why self-justification is more powerful and more dangerous than the explicit lie. It allows people to convince themselves that what they did was the best thing they could have done.

It's possible to overcome the influence of false information just like it is possible to deconvert from a cult. But it's also difficult. It means going against our nature, and disregarding impulses that made us who we are today. Avoiding junk news—or being able to recognize it and disregard it when you do see it—means swimming upstream to safety while the rushing waters of evolution, advertising, and politics push against you. It's not easy, but it's an incredibly important practice, nonetheless.

Regardless of *why* people cling to the term "fake news" as a defense mechanism, one thing is clear: to do so can fuel the war on the media.

4 The War on the Media

> *"The crisis we face about 'truth' and reliable facts is predicated less on the ability to get people to believe the *wrong* thing as it is on the ability to get people to *doubt* the right thing."*
>
> —Jamais Cascio, author

Whatever we all think about politics, religion, etc., most people can agree on one thing: there's a serious problem with the mainstream media (that is *not* to say fringe media is any better—it is absolutely *not*). Does that mean that journalists are the "enemy," as some would suggest? Not even a little bit. But it *does* mean that there is at least a public concern with how journalists *appear* to be operating. In fact, studies have shown a consistent decline in public confidence in the news media. Most U.S. adults and more than 9 in 10 Republicans say they lost trust in the news, according to a 2018 Gallup poll (Knight Foundation, 2018).

There are *legitimate* concerns about how the media operates, and I'll be bringing those to your attention throughout this book, but there's also a *war* on journalism that has nothing to do with the facts at hand. And there are two major contributors to this war: those who are aware of what they're doing and those who are unwittingly contributing to the problem.

"Lying Press"

First, I'd like to focus on those who intentionally deride the media for their own personal gain. This has been a common tactic throughout history, especially for dictators who hoped to suppress negative reports that were based in reality. Consider again the German word *Lügenpresse*, an antijournalist pejorative that dates back nearly a hundred years and is still being used to this day. Literally meaning "lying press," *Lügenpresse* has been used throughout Germany for decades to attack a variety of journalist targets, including all foreign media during the First World War (SPIEGEL Staff, 2016).

But it wasn't all about *attacking* the press; they also wanted to create a "media" of their own. In that sense, Hitler himself is known for pioneering the modern propaganda campaign. The notorious dictator began a job as an army propagandist in 1919, and continued to use those skills for the rest of his life, according to an opinion piece published by the *New York Times* (Snyder, 2019):

> Hitler's form of politics gained mass support when the Great Depression brought to Germany a new series of global shocks. One of the consequences of that economic crisis (as of the one of 2008) was the collapse of independent newspapers, an institution Hitler always denounced as a Jewish "enemy of the people." As the voices of journalists were weakened, the propagandists delivered the coup de grâce. By then, Hitler and the Nazis had found the simple slogan they repeated again and again to discredit reporters: "Lügenpresse."

If this all sounds familiar to you, there's a good reason for that. This is exactly the same tactic used by those across the political spectrum who hope to censor *legitimate* news reports by labelling them as mere "fake news" in order to prop up a fraudulent narrative. This is a method that millions of people engage in, and the worst *providers* of actual misinformation are guilty. If you think I'm exaggerating, just look at this tweet by noted conspiracy theorist Alex Jones, who has claimed the government is using chemicals to turn people and frogs gay. Jones has become synonymous with baseless conspiracy theories, yet he accused Hillary Clinton and NBC anchor Brian Williams of being "notorious for #fakenews."

As the quote at the beginning of this chapter suggests, *this* is the most important battle in the war on fake news. Those who *intentionally proliferate* misinformation do so for a few reasons: to promote an agenda, for more clicks and income, or to troll a group. These are relatively easy to identify and stop.

But those who seek to attack the media itself, attempting to get people to doubt the facts, do so for one sinister reason: to undermine an institution that reveals information. They do this to protect themselves, or perhaps to shield unethical political figures they admire. Or perhaps they've been brainwashed by someone with those motives.

This is a point that has been made by John Yarmuth, an U.S. politician and former newspaper editor:

> If you destroy the credibility of those people or institutions
> that could undermine your own, you create an opportunity
> for your voice, however irresponsible or misleading it may be,
> to gain traction.

In short, if you can effectively silence press inquiries, you can get away with just about anything.

That is further confirmed by Serbian investigative journalist Stevan Dojčinović, who accepted the Knight International Journalism Award from the International Center for Journalists in 2019. He said Serbia is a good case study for understanding how autocrats can use undermining the media as a means to dismantling an entire democracy (Dorroh, 2019):

> The first goal of autocrats is to undermine the media. We journalists are the last threat to organized crime and corruption. And the nail that sticks up gets pounded down hardest.

That is true. Attacks on the press affect journalists a lot in terms of their credibility, but that's not all we have to worry about in terms of rippling damage.

Effects of War on Media

The continual attacks on the press by politicians and commentators alike, including referring to reporters as "the enemy of the people," haven't been without impact. In 2019, the United States dropped three spots to 48 out of 180 on a list that ranks countries according to press freedom, from most to least. This puts our nation in a grouping with others that have "a noticeably problematic press freedom environment," according to a Reporters without Borders report (Reporters without Borders, 2019).

That same report found that the barrage of undermining language used toward reporters has actually caused an increase in violence against members of the press as well. In addition, because of the war on media, reporters have been charged as criminals throughout the world for merely doing their job. In the United States alone, eight journalists faced criminal charges going into 2018, according to the Radio Television Digital

News Association. One of those journalists was Priscilla Villar-eal of Laredo, Texas, who was reportedly charged with "misuse of official information" while covering border patrol (RTDNA, 2018). In other places around the world, things are much worse. In 2019, the number of journalists imprisoned for doing their job remained at record highs internationally, according to a survey by the Committee to Protect Journalists, which listed China, Turkey, Saudi Arabia, and Egypt as the worst jailers of journalists (Beiser, 2019).

Regardless of how you feel about today's journalists, it's clear that an independent and capable media is the enemy of any corrupt individual. And it's equally obvious that, whether you use the term "*Lügenpresse*," "fake news," or something else, delegitimizing news journalism *itself* isn't the answer. We have to *reform* the media so that it works as well as it possibly can.

It is partly because of these rampant verbal attacks and the resulting distrust that the media finds itself in the position of being in the line of fire, sometimes literally. When you're a jour-nalist, many people in the world hate you for just doing your job and looking for the truth. And things only appear to be getting worse with time, leading to violence.

Violence and Threats

Among other issues, the aforementioned "war" on the media makes being a journalist a dangerous gig, and there isn't often a huge slate of benefits to make up for that fact.

The most obvious threat facing journalists today is the threat of *death* from people who have demonized the media or who otherwise want to stop the truth from getting out. While these types of threats and attacks have been on the rise in recent years, there is nothing explicitly *new* about them. In the nine-teenth century, for instance, attacks on the press were "common" in large part due to "the partisan politics most newspapers propagated," according to a report from the *Conversation* (Moore & Socolow, 2018):

> Abolitionist and newspaper editor Elijah Lovejoy was murdered in Alton, Illinois, in 1837. A pro-slavery mob broke into his jail cell—where he had been placed for his protection—and lynched him. One year earlier, in New York City, The New York Herald's James Gordon Bennett was savagely beaten by his rival, James Watson Webb. Webb edited New York City's best-selling newspaper, The Morning Courier and New-York Enquirer, and he'd grown tired of Bennett's attacks in his popular newspaper column. When Ida B. Wells-Barnett published anti-lynching reports in Memphis in 1892, a white mob destroyed her press and threatened to kill her.

Although attacks on the media have existed for hundreds of years, the first event that comes to my mind is the *Charlie Hebdo* shooting in January 2015. Instead of being prompted by a hatred for the media in general, this attack was carried out by members of a radical Islamic group in retaliation for cartoons depicting the Muslim prophet, Muhammad. Still, it had a chilling effect on the journalism industry. And it normalized the behavior that would follow, such as in 2018, when Jarrod Ramos killed five people in the *Capital Gazette* newsroom in Annapolis, Maryland. Ramos had a history of litigation with the paper based on their reporting of his harassment conviction, but his lawsuit was thrown out because he was unable to identify any part of their article that was false (Tavernise, Harmon, & Salam, 2018).

These issues exist even in countries known for having strong democracies and journalistic freedom, such as Sweden. One study found that 33 percent of journalists surveyed there experienced threats at work in the year prior. The researchers wrote in the abstract (Nilsson & Örnebring, 2016):

> Intimidation and harassment also had consequences, both professionally and personally, such as fear and self-censorship. We therefore argue that it is time to add the dimension of external pressure and threats to the discussion of journalistic autonomy—including in countries like Sweden.

For some reporters who write about less controversial news items, they may not be killed tomorrow, but journalists across nearly every industry are subjected to personal insults and the occasional threats of outward violence. This even extends to female sports reporters, who are often harassed. In addition to that regular problem, women in sports media were met with a bigger flood of sexist insults over their coverage of the World Cup, according to European reports (Rat, 2019).

No matter where journalists live or what they write about, there is a certain amount of risk that comes with the job. Unfortunately, that risk has grown in recent years, and it shows no sign of slowing down. All we can do is try to channel our energy into something more positive.

Positive Pushback

Believe it or not, there are possible benefits to the global war against journalism. For example, despite reporters being normally competitive separatists by their very nature,[6] direct attacks against the media have been shown to prompt a type of cooperation that is seldom seen in the field.

Jonathan Rauch, senior fellow of governance studies at the

---

6. This is an issue that I'll discuss in chapter 10.

Brookings Institution, took that even further in asking whether a war on "fake news" could make mainstream media stronger.

"Nixon and Watergate wounded up strengthening the institutions that Nixon hated the most, mainstream media chief among them," he wrote, explaining that the same effect could be achieved in modern times.

In addition to the newfound levels of cooperation when journalists are together in the proverbial foxhole, some have researched monetary incentives associated with the "war."

While it cannot be denied that persistent attacks on the media have been shown by some accounts to have successfully reduced the public's confidence in news reports (Rutenberg, 2018), studies also suggest major news networks have benefited financially from attacks leveled against them. One staff writer at the *Atlantic* found that many news networks that are heavily steeped in political content saw improvements when they should have experienced declines (Thompson, 2017):

> Pay TV is in structural decline, as younger viewers cut the cord or never subscribe in the first place. But the three major cable-news networks have each set viewership records in the first 100 days of Trump's presidency. Fox News had the best quarter in cable news history. MSNBC grew more than 50 percent in both daytime and primetime. CNN also saw double-digit growth over its sensational 2016 ratings. Feeding off the fumes of Trump's whirling-dervish presidency, the networks seem to be growing at the expense of practically everything else on television.

Thompson made a similar point in terms of print media, pointing out that the *New York Times* had recently announced a record growth for digital subscriptions. Other newspapers, the report says, had also experienced a boost in subscriptions due to the attacks and heightened degree of drama.

So, you might be asking, is it all worth it? The answer is simply, "No." No amount of positive benefits would be worth the casualties—whether it's human lives or human rights—that we've experienced in the war on media. Despite that fact, it never hurts to focus on positive ways to improve our situation, instead of what's going wrong in our world.

While violence and threats against reporters, an all-time high distrust in news media, and other factors may make you want to give up on journalism entirely, it's crucial that we not allow that to happen and instead help journalism regain its former glory. I don't say this as a journalist, but as someone who lives in society and has seen first-hand the important role such work has played. It might help for journalism to get back to its roots in exposing corruption, although that presents its own challenges.

The Purpose of Journalism

There is an old saying that goes, "Journalism is printing what someone else does not want printed; everything else is public relations." In that way, the war against the media makes some sense, because journalism is inherently confrontational. What I mean by that is that it exists *for the sole purpose* of causing some controversy through the revelation of information that someone doesn't want to see the light of day. To understand this, it may help to *define* investigative journalism.

According to the Investigative Journalism Manual project, investigative journalism can be defined as "a form of journalism in which reporters go in-depth to investigate a single story that may uncover corruption, review government politics or corporate houses, or draw attention to social, economic, political or cultural trends." As many journalists will tell you, this process is also called "*speaking truth to power.*"

As you can see, the goal of this form of journalism is simple: uncover something that someone in power doesn't want you to report on. It's pretty clear why certain political leaders would want to deride this practice, and even why their followers might go along with it, but it is completely unwarranted when we're talking about a thorough investigation bringing out facts. Something that poses as investigative journalism and reports demonstrable falsehoods, of course, is another story.

Because of this necessarily controversial aspect of journalism, it's common for individuals to believe journalists only want to tear people down for their own benefit. They might think reporters are solely focused on attacking politicians in power, and that they aren't doing it for a good reason, but that could just be an issue with communicating journalistic intent. There's a difference between an attack dog and a watchdog, according to Joy Mayer, the founder of Trusting News.

"Power should not go unchecked, across the political spectrum," she told me in an interview. "Taxpayer dollars fund government and someone needs to be paying attention to whether those dollars and whether the public trust is being treated with the respect that it needs, and whether people have been following all the rules."

In order to counteract this assumption that journalists have bad intentions, they should consider being as transparent as possible, and talking more about their motivations for writing the story, according to Mayer. "If we are working on behalf of the people, we need to state that clearly," she explained.

Mayer also said the assumption that reporters are driven by a personal agenda, as well as other common concerns about journalists, are true in some cases. There are "a lot of irresponsible things done in the name of journalism," according to Mayer.

"It's true somewhere, so the skepticism on the part of the public is 100 percent true and valid," Mayer said in explaining how journalists should view complaints.

In order to compensate for those negative views, reporters should show their process as clearly as possible, allowing readers to "follow the breadcrumbs" along with them, Mayer said.

The focus on misconduct by powerful individuals is something that causes concern, but it isn't the only thing that draws skepticism from readers.

Anonymous Sources

One of the most common targets in the war on the media, the cannon fodder, is the use of anonymous sources. And it makes sense if you think about the simple fact that *most people don't know what goes into sourcing* in general. Many antipress politicians will bring up anonymous sources in their rants against the media, saying reporters are simply making these sources up, but that couldn't be further from the truth. In fact, the process of sourcing in traditional journalism is quite extensive, and anonymous sourcing often requires multiple levels of verification and support from editors. That means that these "anonymous sources" are anything but anonymous to the newsroom that they're working with.

More than that, anonymous sources are a consistent target because they are often the *most important sources*, the ones closest to the powerful individual, corporation, or government. They are the people who would be harmed most by speaking out, so they hide their information in order to help expose some wrongdoing while preserving a sense of normalcy in their daily lives. Here's an explanation from the Society of Professional Journalists (SPJ):

Anonymous sources are sometimes the only key to unlocking a big story, throwing back the curtain on corruption, fulfilling the journalistic missions of watchdog on the government and informant to citizens. But sometimes, anonymous sources are the road to the ethical swamp.

What critics won't tell you is that this aforementioned ethical swamp can be avoided by (1) using anonymous sources as the last resort and (2) following internal controls involving verification and motive questioning.

Research shows that some people truly believe "anonymous sources" are completely anonymous, even to the reporters themselves, according to Joy Mayer. But that isn't even close to being true. She said some newsrooms have started using the phrase "unnamed source" instead, to show that they are *known* but that their name is being withheld for a very specific reason.

"There are plenty of people who think we just make things up, and the problem here is we don't have a counter-narrative too often," Mayer said in an interview. "We wish people didn't think that, but we're not out there correcting the record. We need to be correcting the record every single place we have people's attention."

Mayer said the most important thing to look for when it comes to reporters and unnamed sources is whether they have a consistent and transparent policy for utilizing such individuals. Newsrooms need to have specific plans that address these issues, and they need to be as up front as possible about it.

When a journalist *does* use unnamed sources, they should explain that it was in accordance with ethics policies and then link to said policies, Mayer added.

Educating the public about anonymous sourcing, using it only in strict accordance with a well-maintained policy, and communicating that process to readers are all key factors to correcting misconceptions about unnamed sources that have led to confusion and media distrust. But there is a *lot* more to it than that.

5 Society Fights Back

"We must all hang together, or, most assuredly,
we shall all hang separately."

—Benjamin Franklin, U.S. Founding Father

Now we know we are evolutionarily predisposed to believing information with which we agree, and that people and corporations generate an immense amount of content aimed at exploiting this fact and reinforcing our false ideas. So, why is it important to fight back? Well, for starters, we want to improve our own lives. By challenging our ideas and remaining skeptical of unverified reports, we can train our brain and improve our fact-finding skills, which can prevent us from being tricked as easily. This also reduces the amount of cognitive dissonance we feel, which makes our lives better.

On a broader scale, solving the fake news problem can help us avoid a real-world *Idiocracy*—a society in which the most gullible and the least informed control the government (and just about everything else). This type of future is actually possible, especially considering that believing one piece of false information can make people more likely to believe in others. If nothing is done, and the trend of apathy regarding veracity continues, a humanity that doesn't value facts or knowledge is foreseeable. If we fight back, however, we could do something truly great instead.

Pushing Back Against Misinformation

The degradation of journalism and rise of fake news haven't gone unnoticed. There has actually been a lot of pushback from a society that doesn't want to be dragged down by misinformation. A lot of this pressure from the public has forced the hand of social media companies.

Facebook, for instance, has taken steps to limit the influence of clickbait and misinformation. The social media giant announced in 2019 that it would update its algorithm so that fewer unwanted ads and clickbait articles show up in consumers' newsfeeds. That same year, the company announced it would work with global news agency Agence France-Presse to review veracity of posts (although that program started out only in Malaysia). Even a year earlier, Facebook reportedly paid millions for an artificial-intelligence company that targets fake news content (O'Hear, 2018). In fact, Facebook has been taking on nuanced efforts since 2016, and those efforts have paid off, according to one study:

> User interactions with false content rose steadily on both Facebook and Twitter through the end of 2016. Since then, however, interactions with false content have fallen sharply on Facebook while continuing to rise on Twitter, with the ratio of Facebook engagements to Twitter shares decreasing by 60 percent. In comparison, interactions with other news,

business, or culture sites have followed similar trends on both platforms. Our results suggest that Facebook's efforts to limit the diffusion of misinformation after the 2016 election may have had a meaningful impact.

There are certainly positive results to consider here, but Facebook has had a series of mishaps in this area as well. In fact, in November 2019, a report showed that fake political news was actually still on the rise on the social media site well into the 2020 presidential election season (Associated Press, 2019).

Some critics have also complained that the company selectively censors certain viewpoints, and others have said its efforts to provide users with a "secret trustworthiness score" don't go far enough (Coen, 2018).

In fact, Facebook itself announced in September 2019 that it would allow politicians to lie in ads. The disclosure came as a company official was outlining efforts it was taking to prevent foreign forces from using the platform to undermine elections in the United States.

Nick Clegg, Facebook's vice president of global affairs and communications, said:

> We have a responsibility to protect the platform from outside interference, and to make sure that when people pay us for political ads we make it as transparent as possible. But it is not our role to intervene when politicians speak. That's why I want to be really clear today—we do not submit speech by politicians to our independent fact-checkers, and we generally allow it on the platform even when it would otherwise breach our normal content rules.

While Facebook seems to be making some (inconsistent) efforts, it is clear the company has no intention of *stopping* fake news on its platform. The company said as much when it banned noted conspiracy theorist Alex Jones on August 6, 2018. Officials went out of their way to make it clear that his proliferation of fake news had nothing to do with their decision to ban him (Facebook, 2018):

> People can say things on Facebook that are wrong or untrue, but we work to limit the distribution of inaccurate information. We partner with third-party fact checkers to review and rate the accuracy of articles on Facebook. When something is rated as false, those stories are ranked significantly lower in News Feed, cutting future views by more than 80%.

To make matters worse, Facebook moderators in charge of determining inappropriate content are in some cases adopting the faulty fringe views found in videos they should be throttling, according to the company's stated policies. That finding was buried in a 2019 profile of American Facebook moderators, which found that "the conspiracy videos and memes that they see each day gradually lead them to embrace fringe views," such as Flat-Eartherism (Newton, 2019b):

> One auditor walks the floor promoting the idea that the Earth is flat. A former employee told me he has begun to question certain aspects of the Holocaust. Another former employee, who told me he has mapped every escape route out of his house and sleeps with a gun at his side, said: "I no longer believe 9/11 was a terrorist attack."

To summarize: 9/11 conspiracy theories, Holocaust denial, and Flat Earth beliefs are all being spread at this one location for Facebook content moderators.

This is something I've never really thought about, but it

does make sense that viewing controversial content regularly could lead to some changes in beliefs over time. It has been said that, if people see or hear anything enough times, it becomes believable to some. That's due to the *illusory truth effect*, which describes why false statements that are repeated are "perceived to be more truthful" than novel statements that are actually true, according to a study published in the *Journal of Experimental Psychology* (Fazio, Payne, Brashier, & Marsh, 2015). That same study found that having *knowledge* about the subjects doesn't protect against the effect. The researchers wrote:

> Contrary to prior suppositions, illusory truth effects occurred even when participants knew better. Multinomial modeling demonstrated that participants sometimes rely on fluency even if knowledge is also available to them. Thus, participants demonstrated knowledge neglect, or the failure to rely on stored knowledge, in the face of fluent processing experiences.

Identifying how these false beliefs spread will be critical to the human race eventually overcoming them and improving public education around the world. If we don't understand the problem, we'll never come up with a solution, so insights like this are always important to me. But that is for long-term solutions. What do we do in the meantime?

One method for reducing the negative consequences associated with dangerous fake news in the short term has little to do with *understanding* it and everything to do with avoiding it.

Limiting Access to Fake News

While Facebook is making some attempts to reduce the influence of misinformation, many companies and governments are not doing *anything* at all when it comes to combatting the spread of dangerous fake news. They will have to be dragged kicking and screaming into the real world.

Consider the "documentary" *Vaxxed*, a popular film that promotes the debunked autism-vaccine connection, and how it was available and being promoted by Amazon Prime as recently as 2019. I personally protested the video's presence and status on the Prime platform, but it wasn't until Rep. Adam Schiff (D-CA) wrote a letter that anything was done. The California official said recommending the film to Prime users was "reversing progress made in tackling vaccine-preventable diseases." In the 2019 letter, Schiff wrote:

> As the largest online marketplace in the world, Amazon is in a unique position to shape consumption. The algorithms which power social media platforms and Amazon's recommendations are not designed to distinguish quality information from misinformation or misleading information and, as a result, harmful anti-vaccine messages have been able to thrive and spread. The consequences are particularly troubling for public health issues.

Amazon ultimately pulled the film from its platform following pressure from legislators, but that didn't stop the makers of *Vaxxed* from bringing the world a sequel, called *Vaxxed II: The People's Truth*, in November 2019. In fact, the producers of the film, including Robert F. Kennedy Jr., cast the removal from Prime as an issue of "censorship," and used it to drum up more viewers. The *Vaxxed* sequel wasn't released on any of the major streaming sites, but it was screened at "secret" showings in theaters across the country, purportedly in an attempt to avoid being blocked once again (Gander, 2019).

Amazon may have eventually decided to ban the potentially

dangerous antiscience film, but others are still on various streaming services. It remains clear that corporations themselves can't be solely trusted with the responsibility of limiting fake news.

YouTube is another company with spotty performance in terms of stopping deadly fake news. In February 2019, BuzzFeed News reported that the video platform was promoting and recommending antivaccination propaganda amid a measles outbreak across the country, despite Facebook taking steps to limit similar content (O'Donovan & McDonald, 2019).

Two days after the BuzzFeed report, YouTube announced that it was demonetizing antivaccination channels (O'Donovan, "YouTube Just Demonetized Anti-Vax Channels," 2019). But does that reactionary move mean the company is committed to limiting the prevalence of pseudoscience with the potential to cause harm? Well, if that's the case, its actions haven't done much to show it.

For example, the video platform, along with Facebook and Apple, also famously banned Alex Jones, but it did so for "hate speech" and not for potentially dangerous fake news. The popular video site has also become known for its enabling of the Flat Earther movement, which has a belief system that relies on a conspiracy between all of NASA and every major government agency around the globe. Researchers at Texas Tech University attended two of the world's largest Flat Earth gatherings and interviewed the people at both pseudoscientific conferences. The results pointed to one commonality: YouTube. Their work found that a huge number—almost 100 percent—of Flat Earthers were convinced of their current beliefs thanks to YouTube. But it's not a bug, it's a function, according to the researchers (Olshansky, 2018):

> Indeed, many people were introduced to Flat Earth theories through YouTube: after watching other conspiracy videos,

the site's algorithms led to suggestions of more conspiracy videos, which included those about Flat Earth. . . . It seems increasingly plausible that in the age of YouTube and in the wake of 9/11, Biblical literalists with a penchant for conspiracy ideation, who began as consumers of 9/11 conspiracy videos, were steered toward other conspiracy videos, including flat Earth videos, as a result of YouTube's algorithms.

Basically, because of the way the site works, YouTube could be *creating* Flat Earthers and spreading all sorts of unverified beliefs that have the potential to cause harm.

For another example of YouTube endorsing dangerous misinformation, we need to look back no further than October 2019, about eight months after the company was pushed to demonetize antivaccination clips, when it promoted its chiropractic videos to its 72.1 million followers on Twitter. The "cracking" videos appear to be incredibly popular on YouTube, which could be why it wanted to draw even more attention to them with a tweet.

The company hailed its clips featuring bone adjustments, saying they deserve more recognition. "[C]ould listen to those skeletal cracks for HOURS," YouTube tweeted.

Regardless of the company's intentions, several activists and Twitter users had a problem with the promotion of chiropractic, a process invented by a "magnetic healer" and salesman who believed it could cure just about *anything*, including deafness. The practice is considered by many to be a pseudoscience and it is responsible for several deaths. Among those killed is Katie May, a model who passed away in 2016 following an injury caused by a chiropractic adjustment. Specifically, she was killed by a vertebral artery dissection, according to CBS News (CBS News, 2016):

Days before the 34-year-old died in February, she posted on Twitter that she'd pinched a nerve in her neck at a photo-shoot and was going to visit a chiropractor. Friends said she became sick a few hours after her appointment and was taken to the emergency room. She was pronounced brain dead the next day and taken off life support.

. . . .

'This is actually more common than people think—that people get over-adjusted and there's a tear and it causes a stroke and death," said Ronald Richards, Katie May estate's lawyer.

These accidental deaths, along with the fact that studies have shown chiropractic to be no more effective than other physical manipulation therapies like massage, have led some researchers to conclude that its risks outweigh the benefits (Ernst, 2010).

In the past, YouTube has also allowed videos to be hosted that promote ideas considered by the government to be dangerous, including drinking a bleaching agent thought by some to cure autism and basically every other condition, even if it did keep the creators from directly making money from them. The platform announced an apparent end to this policy in 2019, creating a new category to report what the company now calls "harmful treatments" (McAfee, 2019).

Google, which owns YouTube, has similarly been criticized for promoting misinformation while at the same time taking some steps toward limiting access to those postings. In 2017, for instance, Google began facing accusations regarding its "featured" search options, which were said to contain conspiracy theories and misinformation in some rare instances. The Google feature, which is supposed to pull from popular sites to lead searchers in the right direction quickly, ended up spreading "fake news" to many curious readers instead. In responding to the controversy, Google said this was an accidental byproduct of its algorithmic approach and promised to "work quickly to remove" featured items containing fake news (Hern, 2017).

Unfortunately for Google, that wasn't the end of its woes regarding its alleged promotion of fake news. On November 20, 2019, the company announced that it was limiting political advertisers' ability to target people online and to make false claims in ads. This was in response to criticisms that the company, along with Facebook, ran purposefully misleading ads for Donald Trump's presidential campaign (Bergen, 2019).

For its part, Google framed the change as a clarification of its existing policies. Scott Spencer, vice president of product management for Google Ads, wrote in a corporate blog post:

> It's against our policies for any advertiser to make a false claim—whether it's a claim about the price of a chair or a claim that you can vote by text message, that election day is postponed, or that a candidate has died. To make this more explicit, we're clarifying our ads policies and adding examples to show how our policies prohibit things like "deep fakes" (doctored and manipulated media), misleading claims about the census process, and ads or destinations making demonstrably false claims that could significantly undermine participation or trust in an electoral or democratic process.

Twitter is another platform on which fake news, including dangerous conspiracy theories with violent themes, seems to spread without abatement. Twitter claims to have cracked down on *bots* that spread fake news, but that has left the human element untouched. And even its work regarding automated accounts that push spam has been called into question by a study that found 82 percent of the malicious bots that worked in the 2016 election were still active years later (Hindman & Barash, 2018).

Potential Government Solutions

If you're thinking that corporations themselves can't possibly be responsible for solving this problem completely alone, because they aren't known as ethical touchstones and have very little incentive to truly attempt such a feat, you are right. There are other concerns with the corporate approach, as well. Our society is outsourcing these solutions to "private entities that exist, ultimately, to make a profit and not necessarily for a social good," according to Sally Wentworth, vice president of global policy development at the Internet Society. "How much power are we turning over to them . . . ? Do we know where that might eventually lead?" she asks.

Some elected officials have taken the issue into their own hands. In Germany, lawmakers took a direct approach to harmful false reports, enacting a social media law that prohibits spreading fake news that incites hate. That measure came after a series of fake news stories perpetuating hate for immigrants went viral (Faiola & Kirchner, 2017). In 2018, Germany began enforcing its law banning hate speech, fake news, and illegal material (BBC, 2018). A year later, a Facebook subsidiary was fined about $2.2 million for not properly completing a transparency report (Gesley, 2019). The UK politician Damian Collins, Conservative MP for Folkestone and Hythe, floated the idea of creating new regulations for social media companies (Collins, 2018):

> We believe that by creating new legal liabilities for social media companies to act against known sources of harmful and misleading content, it is more likely that they will do so. We are going to need the tech companies to do more to help us combat threats like these.

Government officials across the world have at least pondered the notion of stopping misinformation. In fact, at the time of writing, laws that (at least in name) address fake news have been enacted or considered in several nations, including Singapore, France, Malaysia, the European Union, China, and even Russia[7] (Ungku, 2019). In Singapore, officials issued their first-ever correction request in November 2019 under a "fake news" law that allows for monitoring and correction of misinformation (Reuters, 2019).

Another unique solution was proposed by Boston University information economist Marshall Van Alstyne, who suggested a plan inspired by economist Arthur Pigou. Under that system, officials would enact a fee to deter a negative behavior, sometimes called a "sin tax." Van Alstyne said (Lennon, 2019):

> You could sample messages, find out some proportion of false and damning information, and then tax in proportion to the damage that's being done. What you're doing is you're taxing the damage. You're not taxing the speech.

Additionally, the state of California considered its own governmental approach to the problem of misinformation, with legislators passing a bill in 2018 that would have created a "fake news" advisory group to monitor how faulty news reports spread online. Senate Bill 1424 would have required the creation of a committee made up of social media representatives, rights advocates, and members of the U.S. Department of Justice (Yurus, 2018).

That plan was ultimately shut down with a veto by California's then governor, Jerry Brown (D), who held that the measure was "not necessary," stating (Good Day Sacramento, 2018):

---

7. It's important to note that, in some cases, dictators and authoritarian regimes can enact laws that limit free speech under the guise of fighting fake news.

This bill directs the Attorney General to establish an advisory group to study the problem of the spread of false information through Internet-based social media platforms. As evidenced by the numerous studies by academic and policy groups on the spread of false information, the creation of a statutory advisory group to examine this issue is not necessary.

I don't know anyone who thinks government alone can solve the fake news problem in its entirety, but there's no telling what interventions could be a part of the solution, so it's important that they be considered.

Still, there could be other solutions that hit even closer to the root of the issue.

Financial Disincentivization

One common thread among many of the possible solutions described so far is that they involve the financial disincentivization of false information, particularly the misinformation posted online. I think this could potentially be a valuable component of the overall solution, because monetary compensation is *one* huge motivator for fake news. For many blogs and online media sources, the author is paid per click, which is one reason for this situation we find ourselves in. That's not to say that *every* click-based operation is inherently bad, of course, but the system itself does open the floodgates for abuse.

Companies know that generating clicks is what gets them paid, so it's only natural that they will want to do what they can to increase the number of people who are interested enough to click a button. (They don't *always* care how much of the article you read, although the time you linger on a page is also measured and likely taken into consideration by many corporations.) The natural result of this is that people and corporate entities will use deceptive images, exaggerated headlines, and untrue implications in order to increase their metrics and make more money. Sometimes these underhanded tactics fit within the law, and other times they don't.

Right now, there is an "incentive to spread fake news," according to Amber Case, research fellow at Harvard's Berkman Klein Center for Internet & Society:

> It is profitable to do so, profit made by creating an article that causes enough outrage that advertising money will follow. In order to reduce the spread of fake news, we must disincentivize it financially.

If we can find ways to undermine the system that enables and encourages fake news, perhaps by disallowing royalties for fake news–based media content, eliminating certain tax breaks for companies that spread false information, or otherwise levying fines against those who push dangerous fake news for their own financial benefit, maybe we can change the information landscape for the better.

This financial disincentivization plan wouldn't *solve* the problems that we're experiencing, though. It would be a Band-Aid to help stop the bleeding, but it doesn't get to *all* the causes of fake news and its immense success in modern times. It's not a solution in itself, because working to eliminate the monetary aspect wouldn't heal the injury. It could, however, be used with a variety of other measures to bring some relief from our wounds and keep them from getting much worse.

Technological Answers

If platforms on which misinformation spreads most often can't regulate themselves, and governments fail to intervene or to do so adequately, then it is up to innovators to help create techno-logical solutions that at least reduce the amount of faulty re-ports internet users come into contact with.

As far as apps and programs go, there are many aimed at preventing the spread of "fake news." They aren't equally ef-fective, though. Here I'll discuss a few of the top tech solutions, how the programs work, and whether they might function in tandem with other proposals to curb misinformation that hurts people.

- **Video games**. Yes, you read that right: playing video games can help break your dependence on "fake news." I'm talking specifically about apps and puzzle games created with the specific purpose of retraining your gullible brain. This isn't just a hypothetical idea I'm pitching, either; there are already several of these on the market. There is Politi-Truth, a mobile game created by PolitiFact; Fake News: The Game, by ISL; and Factitious, a game created by a former *Los Angeles Times* correspondent (Schmidt, 2017).

- **SurfSafe**. This app (an extension to the Chrome internet browser) searches only for image repetition, so it isn't a solu-tion to all fake news. That said, it could be helpful to know when and where images you're seeing have been used be-fore, especially since so many sources of faulty reports recy-cle images from legitimate news stories. SurfSafe's site says:

  > SurfSafe uses the news sites you trust, along with fact-checking pages and user reports as benchmarks for what images are considered 'safe'. It's simple—just hover over an image, and SurfSafe will classify the image as 'safe', 'warning', or 'unsafe'. SurfSafe will also show you every instance of where the image in question has been seen before.

- **Other Chrome extensions.** In addition to SurfSafe, there are several other Chrome extensions that can help users detect fake news. Another option is FiB: Stop living a lie, a student-created app that was developed at a Princeton University hackathon event (Bort, 2016). FiB is supposed to check pictures, text, and embedded links and flag them for misinformation. Other Chrome extensions along similar lines include BS Detector and Fake News Detector.

- **Cheq.** This is a tech start-up working on demonetizing "fake news" using military-grade technology. The company hopes to prevent advertisers from making buys on certain content, including misinformation. CNBC reports (Graham, 2019):

  > In the lead-up to the 2020 presidential election, Cheq is using artificial intelligence to try to identify fake news and make sure brands and agencies don't place ads on them.

- **Machine learning.** Of the numerous proposed solutions to the "fake news" problem, a select few software solutions emphasize machine learning. For instance, the Fraunhofer Institute in Germany put forth a plan to teach a program how to pick up on the subtle differences between traditional news stories and those pieces that are intentionally false or misleading, using the articles' content and metadata. The institute cast the tool as a "useful early warning system," according to a press announcement (Research News, 2019). Professor Ulrich Schade of Fraunhofer said:

  > Our software focuses on Twitter and other websites. Tweets are where you find the links pointing to the web pages that contain the actual fake news. In other words, social media acts as a trigger, if you like. Fake news items are often hosted on websites designed to mimic the web

presence of news agencies and can be difficult to distinguish from the genuine sites. In many cases, they will be based on official news items, but in which the wording has been altered.

Researchers at Fraunhofer have also studied how to identify "fake images," which accompany fake news items, using an application for feature detection. This method, researchers said, would be "an alternative to image forensics based on finding traces of splicing" that would "produce better detection results compared to it" (Steinebach, Gotkowski, & Liu, 2019).

Research on similar tactics for using machine learning to detect and stop "fake news" is also being conducted by academics at major institutions such as the Massachusetts Institute of Technology and Harvard. The authors of that study concluded that convolutional neural networks, a class of deep neural networks often used to analyze images, "can be a powerful tool to detect fake news in novel topics, solely from the language (no syntax, semantics or source analysis)" (O'Brien, Latessa, Evangelopoulos, & Boix, 2018).

- **Credibility analysis**. Because so much of fake news boils down to the credibility of the reporters and the news organizations themselves, a start-up called Credder seeks to create a website with ratings based on reviews from journalists and everyday readers alike. The website would allow anyone to check the credibility rating of a particular publication, making it a sort of Rotten Tomatoes for the news world (Ha, 2019).

Tech options are great to have, but no app is going to be the one solution that will solve the rampant misinformation problem our society is currently facing.

Nuanced, Multipronged Approaches

No matter what technology companies employ, and no matter what new applications we devise to limit the spread of harmful fake news online, it will never get to the source of the problem, according to Mike DeVito, a graduate researcher at Northwestern University:

> These are not technical problems; they are human problems that technology simply helped scale, yet we keep attempting purely technological solutions. We can't machine-learn our way out of this disaster, which is actually a perfect storm of poor civics knowledge and poor information literacy.

DeVito's perspective is seemingly boosted by the Reboot Foundation, which is focused on the promotion and encouragement of critical thinking. The president of the foundation said fake news "is a problem for all of us" and that we all have to work together to solve it.

The solution involves "giving young people the tools to think critically" and not the government intervention that has consistently been floated, according to Reboot Foundation president Helen Lee Bouygues (Reboot Foundation, n.d.):

> The solution is education. Specifically, it's about giving people the power of critical thinking. If you're a better thinker, you're a better judge of information, and that's how we will finally beat fake news.

Due to the deeper issues involved in the debate, as well as the complexity and depth of the fake news problem itself, some groups analyzing possible solutions have put forth intricate and expansive plans factoring in issues such as potential harm and free speech. One prong of a fake news fix could include measures specifically focused on content *consumers*, as opposed to the content creator side we have mostly discussed here. Again, these don't address all the root causes as to why fake news is spread, but they may help to stop it in its tracks and make it less effective. One working group organized by Yale put forth dozens of different options along those same lines (Information Society Project and Floyd Abrams Institute for Freedom of Expression, 2017):

> Consumers could be educated about how news information propagates in today's world, the harms of fake news, and how to identify it. Another approach would be to enable the consumer to learn more about the actors and stakeholders in a given story, better understand their affiliations, and to identify and question unverified details. Critical news consumption could be incorporated into school curriculums or promoted through government-sponsored computer and content literacy tools and training programs.

That same group put forward several potential regulatory suggestions, including an accreditation system or a code of conduct for content creators and distributors. Any system like that, the group said, would have to be designed to "avoid it becoming a means of silencing the 'little guys' or a means of promoting government-approved news."

A separate study conducted by a group of experts including Matthew Baum, the Marvin Kalb Professor of Global Communications at Harvard Kennedy School, reached similar conclusions. Addressing the problem of fake news requires a "multidisciplinary effort" that looks at individuals as well as platforms, the researchers found (Lazer, et al., 2018):

Our call is to promote interdisciplinary research to reduce the spread of fake news and to address the underlying pathologies it has revealed. Failures of the U.S. news media in the early 20th century led to the rise of journalistic norms and practices that, although imperfect, generally served us well by striving to provide objective, credible information. We must redesign our information ecosystem in the 21st century. This effort must be global in scope, as many countries, some of which have never developed a robust news ecosystem, face challenges around fake and real news that are more acute than in the United States. More broadly, we must answer a fundamental question: How can we create a news ecosystem and culture that values and promotes truth?

In the end, there is no one solution to this global problem. There will have to be a million different answers all with one goal: educating the public. TV host John Oliver was right when he said:

The most important thing in a functional society is a well-informed public. What we have now is not only uninformed but misinformed masses.

6 Fake News Is Big Business

"Money is in some respects like fire; it is a very excellent servant but a terrible master."

—P. T. Barnum, showman

The term "mainstream media" could be used as a designation for the top news companies, but it can also be used in a derogatory manner. People who deride mainstream media in this way often argue that it can't be a good venue for truth in part because the owners of some news companies are extraordinarily wealthy or are primarily concerned with increasing profits. While this is undoubtedly true to some extent (I'd argue this is how most businesses are), it completely ignores that there isn't really a great alternative in a society based on capitalism. We can step up our efforts to encourage independent investigative journalism, which wouldn't have the same profit-based concerns or potential conflicts of interest, but that's about the extent of it. Government-sourced news has its own issues that are likely worse than those related to for-profit news. Even if you hate the profit-centric emphasis of the mainstream news and decide to abandon mainstream institutions in favor of fringe sites, you should understand that *fake journalism* can be just as influenced by money as legitimate news.

Successful fake news writers can make between $5,000 (Silverman & Alexander, 2016) and $10,000 (Ohlheiser, 2016) or more per month through various advertising programs, making misinformation an extremely lucrative business in the modern era.[8] In fact, a 2019 Global Disinformation Index report estimated that 20,000 sites known for publishing numerous false reports made a total of $235 million in a year (Melford & Fagan, 2019). Considering there are many more than 20,000 misinformation sites, the $235 million number is considered a massive underestimate of the annual profits for the prolific "fake news" industry.

One publisher of fake news sites, Jestin Coler, confirmed in an interview that reports showing ad revenue of $10,000–$30,000 per month for some misinformation maestros were applicable to him as a "ballpark." Coler says they have "several advertisers," including, at one point in time, Google. Google shut down Coler's account under a new company policy, purportedly because of his intentional proliferation of fake news, but he was able to easily "replace them with other advertisers" (All Things Considered, 2016).

In an interview with a reporter for NPR, Coler said (Sydell, 2016):

> There are literally hundreds of ad networks. Literally hundreds. Last week my inbox was just filled everyday with people, because they knew that Google was cracking down—

---

8. You can compare this to the average pay of journalists, which studies show changes depending on region and topic but can sit between $30,000 and $60,000 per year.

hundreds of people wanting to work with my sites. I kind of applaud Google for their steps, although I think what they're doing is kind of random. They don't really have a process in place for identifying these things. I happen to know a very successful site that, as of today, of this morning is still serving Google ads.

Asked if he would have continued publishing the fake news content if it didn't bring in so much money, Coler said the financial incentives weren't "the only motivator" for him:

I do enjoy making a mess of the people that share the content that comes out of our site. It's not just the financial incentive for me. I still enjoy the game I guess.

Changing the Game

I know what you're thinking (and if you aren't thinking this, I'm going to pretend you are for the sake of storytelling): even if some fake news publishers are making money hand over fist, that doesn't have to be a terrible thing, does it? After all, people need to make money. And making money off of fake news might be bad, but it doesn't necessarily mean the misinformation industry is powerful and capable of unilaterally shifting the focus of journalism itself. However, that is exactly what is happening. While the journalism industry has evolved over many generations to include a complex ethical code related to story veracity, trust, and reader transparency, the ad companies haven't. What we are seeing right now is a fake news industry that doesn't value the truth meeting ad firms that feel the same way.

The unholy alliance between advertisers and publishers of misinformation is causing serious changes in how our whole system works. With growing online presences of fake news companies and increasingly invasive ads supported by data-capturing programs, advertising dollars are trending away from traditional media and journalists, and toward "fake news" content. This has had a major impact on the very nature of online advertising and the incentive structure on which media has relied, which threatens the future of quality journalism and even an informed democracy, according to some scholars (Couldry & Turow, 2014). In other words, society is moving in a direction that directly undermines the business model of journalism, which has been key to an informed citizenry.

Other studies have looked into what the journalism and advertising industries could do, both together and separately, to adjust to the new media landscape—or to help correct the growing problem (Braun & Eklund, 2019):

> [T]he present study on the case of ad tech and hoax news appears to support assertions already levied by scholarly critics—that the advertising ecosystem is currently evolving in ways that will force news organizations to either enter into increasingly unconventional (and, perhaps, undesirable) relationships with the advertising industry or to move away from ad-driven business models altogether. Alternatively, news organizations may need to seek relief through policy reforms aimed at charting a third way.

Regardless of what steps the journalism and ad industries take to address these growing concerns, they may not get to the heart of the issues that got us here in the first place. It's possible that the damage has already been done, but that doesn't mean we should stop fighting back in every way we possibly can. It's important to know, however, that it will likely be an uphill battle against the massively successful institutions that have been created by the modern misinformation explosion.

Industry of Pseudoscience

You've probably heard about "Big Pharma," a pejorative reference to the massive profits of certain pharmaceutical companies, but do you know how big of an industry placebo-based natural "remedies" are? Alternative treatments such as acupuncture, chiropractic, and traditional "healers," which may provide some relief but are not capable of *healing* anything, were responsible for almost $34 billion in out-of-pocket spending in a single year in the United States alone in 2007, according to a government report released at the time (Briand, 2009). A more recent report, published on March 6, 2018, found that dietary supplements are a $30 billion industry, with more than 90,000 products on the market (Manson & Bassuk, 2018). That is despite the fact that studies consistently show only a few of these supplements have a narrow medical value.

Crystals, believed by many to heal users from various ailments or "align their energies," are also part of a multi-billion-dollar industry in which individual dealers can make around $40 million in sales each year. Crystals have even been compared to blood diamonds because a heightened demand in part due to a faux wellness boom has led to increasing human rights abuses in potentially deadly mines (McClure, 2019). Again, this is all without any scientific evidence of efficacy beyond placebo.

Even the practice of *reiki* can make lots of money. If you don't know what reiki is, it's a type of "therapy" that purportedly uses a "healing energy" of the hands. In other words, it's nothing. Still, it has been gaining in popularity, and it can be found everywhere, from farmer's markets to operating rooms (Gorski, 2012).

As just one example of someone raking in the dough with reiki, I'd point to Jessica Brodkin of New York. She once worked as an analyst at the CIA, but after leaving that job she started a reiki gig that brings in $108,000 per year. Brodkin, working out of New York City, took up reiki after leaving her CIA job and trying to make it as a stand-up comedian. After racking up thousands of dollars in debt, she discovered the business of fake "energy healing." She reportedly sees twelve clients per week in Manhattan, charging around $229 for most sessions. She has even "healed" celebrities like Emma Stone, according to a news report from CNBC (Martin, 2019).

Lastly, we should consider the story of Lilia, a "breathwork" practitioner who gets paid to basically help people meditate. She's just one of many young people turning toward new age spiritual practices and, in a bittersweet twist, *away from religious fundamentalism*, according to the *Los Angeles Times* (Roy, 2019).

What we're talking about here is the rise of high-powered pseudosciences, something I like to call *Big Bullshit*. And a lot of it is possible because *fake news treatments* are going mainstream.

Going Mainstream

Due to the increased acceptance of pseudoscience in our society, you don't have to go to some out-of-the-way shop filled with crystals to get access to nonsense "treatments" that rip people off. In fact, you don't usually need to go beyond your local pharmacy or grocery store. I learned this for myself when I went into a Rite Aid in early 2018.

While in the retail health giant, I saw a dangerous and pseudoscientific Himalayan salt "Inhealer" that supposedly helps people "breathe easier without chemical inhalers." Chemical inhalers, also known as *medicine*, have been shown to save lives during an asthma attack. The Inhealer, on the other hand, has no scientific backing and has been promoted by Dr. Oz, who is well known for promoting treatments that aren't proven to work. Still, the product was up for sale at a pharmacy where consumers might reasonably be tricked into believing it has a substantial medicinal value.

I first raised this issue on March 13, 2018, when I saw the so-called Inhealer and posted images on social media. Next, I contacted Rite Aid directly to request a statement. After almost a month of waiting for comment, Rite Aid finally got back to me. A company spokesperson told me Rite Aid "offers a variety of products in its store to meet the needs of the customers."

The same representative told me:

> It's important to note that the packaging of the product available in our stores does not have any reference to respiratory ailments and also includes language that states: This product is not intended to diagnose, treat, cure or prevent any disease. Consult a qualified health care provider before using the Inhealer. Further, in the instructions included with the Inhealer, it is noted that product should not be used in the event of respiratory distress or as a replacement of medication.

So, let's look at the facts:

- The package identifies the product as a "CLASS 1 MEDICAL DEVICE" with "adapted for use with Himalayan Salt" in small print.

- The package advertises "100% natural breathing." On what is this claim based? We have no idea.

- The package states that the product "helps remove impurities in the air," which is unproven.

- The package explicitly says the product is used for "relief to aid in better breathing."

- On the product's online bio, the manufacture claims it helps users "breathe easier without chemical inhalers" and provides "relief from the inflammation and discomfort of asthma or allergies."

Rite Aid felt justified in its decision to sell this product, even though it is clearly dangerous. They point to small print on the package saying the product "has not been evaluated by the Food and Drug Administration," but forget that they're supposed to be in the business of wellness. As someone who had a good friend die from an asthma attack, I find it offensive that they would risk that sort of tragedy because this product brings in money.

While this product may not be technically illegal,[9] it's certainly unethical. And to make matters worse, the Inhealer is only one of *many* examples of mainstream pseudoscientific treatments. Those treatments themselves only represent the tip of the iceberg, considering the celebrity mouthpieces who promote them often make even *more* money.

The Downward Spiral of Oz

It's natural to transition from the Inhealer, which Dr. Oz promoted, to Dr. Oz himself. Once recognized as one of the top surgeons in his field, Dr. Oz has since then been frequently criticized for making millions of dollars promoting "psychic mediums" and unproven cures that some say are dangerous. In fact, in 2014, a scientific study revealed that believable or "somewhat believable" evidence supported only 33 percent of the recommendations on *The Dr. Oz Show*. That was compared to a similar televised medical talk show, *The Doctors*, which sat at the 53 per-

---

9. I haven't verified what the instructions inside say and Rite Aid refused to send me a picture.

cent mark for recommendations that were underpinned by at least somewhat believable evidence (Korownyk, et al., 2014). A year after that study was published, a group of ten well-known doctors wrote to Columbia University to challenge Dr. Oz's position as a faculty member, saying the TV doctor promoted "quack treatments and cures in the interest of personal financial gain" (Stelter, 2015). That prompted one thousand more doctors to say they think he should resign from his position at Columbia (Lewis, 2015). That seems like a lot of bad press that might severely damage a legitimate doctor's reputation and financial prospects, right?

That has *not* been the case for Dr. Oz. Reports from 2013 show he had a net worth of about $7 million, and that number has continued to soar as his TV show has persisted and his profile has risen (O'Rourke, 2016). In fact, unbeknownst to the ten doctors who penned the challenge to Dr. Oz's gig at the university, he would ultimately benefit from the stunt, according to *Los Angeles Times* business columnist Michael Hiltzik (Hiltzik, 2015):

> Those who feared that the TV medical show host Dr. Mehmet Oz would only profit from a recent call by a group of 10 doctors for Columbia University to dump him from its faculty have turned out to be absolutely correct. The Oz counterattack unfolded on Thursday and Friday, in a lengthy segment on his show and appearances on some obliging media outlets. As is the case with many of the health recommendations on his popular daytime program, it was deceptive and selective—designed not to inform, but to obfuscate.

The clapback by Dr. Oz included a 1,300-word exclusive op-ed, an interview telling his side of the story to *NBC Nightly News*, a sit-down interview with the *Today Show*, and other opportunities that only served to raise his profile even further.

Hiltzik pointed out that "none of the 10 letter-writers got any of that live air time."

Those events would catapult Dr. Oz to further fame. In 2018, it was reported that Dr. Oz would be joining President Trump's Council on Sport, Fitness, and Nutrition for a term of two years (Belluz, 2018a). And that same year, he won a Daytime Emmy, according to *Forbes* contributor Michael Schein, who hailed Dr. Oz's leadership strategies that don't require the use of dangerous pseudoscience (Schein, 2018).

After all the pushback, Dr. Oz remains incredibly influential and continues to promote questionable items and "treatments" for his own monetary gain.

Paltrow and Goop

There is an even worse offender in the pseudoscience-for-cash game than Dr. Oz out there. In fact, very few companies embody the spirit of *Big Bullshit* as much as Goop, by actress Gwyneth Paltrow. A one-time recipient of *Skeptic Magazine*'s Rusty Razor Award for world's worst pseudoscience (Pritchard, 2018), Paltrow's global "wellness" brand Goop was also forced to pay $145,000 to settle a consumer protection lawsuit over "unsubstantiated" marketing claims for the infamous jade vaginal egg, which the company claimed could "balance hormones" and "regulate menstrual cycles."[10] Goop apparently continued to sell the vaginal eggs, which have been universally panned by gynecologists, after the fine (Belluz, 2018b). That's not all that surprising, though, considering Goop itself has been valued at a quarter-billion dollars (Brodesser-Akner, 2018), even after admittedly making "mistakes that have cost millions of dollars," according to Paltrow (Steig, 2019). Goop definitely knows how

---

10. In addition to the jade eggs, Paltrow's Goop has sold vaginal steamers, coffee enemas, and more.

to make money.

Goop also knows how to appease its base, as evidenced by its reactionary adoption of "for your enjoyment" and "rigorously tested" labels, purportedly in an attempt to promote scientific transparency among its "wellness" products. Unfortunately, the definitions of some of those labels pushed the blame for the unsupported claims away from the company and onto scientists in general. The "ancient modality" marking, for instance, was reserved for practices that are "nearly as old as time" but for which "modern-day research hasn't caught up yet" (Wischhover, 2018). If Goop wanted to be scientifically accurate, they would only include a single label: "Rigorously tested." Everything else should be labeled as "Pseudoscience" or removed from the site.

Of course, Paltrow would likely oppose some of these characterizations, because she once told a reporter that she and the company "disagree" that they are peddling pseudoscientific and unproven "treatments." The subject came up when *BBC Breakfast*'s Charlie Stayt asked Paltrow about the infamous jade vaginal egg and how Goop ended up paying to settle the consumer protection lawsuit alleging false advertising (Stayt, 2018):

STAYT: How do you make sure that things—in the area of medicine, claiming to have health benefits, do what they say?

PALTROW: We have a whole regulatory team in place now, and a science and research team, and that's really what they're dedicated to doing. So, a lot of times we'll find that a third-party product that we sell . . . people make claims about products.

Other than not answering the reporter's question, and not forming a coherent thought, and blaming the problems on third parties instead of her own lack of openness and honesty, Paltrow ignored the simple fact that hiring a "science" team doesn't mean anything unless it's doing its job. And so far that team hasn't stopped Goop from selling a sack of rocks as a "medicine bag," nor has it kept the company from slinging its "mists" for "psychic vampire repellant" and "kid calming."

Stayt pushed further, specifically bringing up the vaginal egg lawsuit that led Goop to pay out more than $100,000. Paltrow's response was lacking there, too. She didn't mention the name of the product, didn't explain what false claims the company made, and leaned heavily on the fact that she didn't "have to admit" any wrongdoing:

> One of the products we sell, some of the regulators in California said, "You can't say that it does that" and so we never had any customer complaints about it at all. But we chose . . . we didn't say . . . we didn't have to admit that we . . . you know . . . any wrongdoing. We just wanted to settle it and put it behind us.

After stuttering her way through an awkward situation, Paltrow insisted this was all just part of growing up as a startup:

> Of course, as you learn and grow, you—especially when you're a startup—you have to learn kind of on the job, unfortunately, a lot of times.

It's true you have to learn on the job. But claiming that psychics are real and that rocks up your vagina can make you healthy is a deliberate choice. Paltrow decided to promote dubious products meant for gullible customers and not to actually improve anyone's well-being.

Stayt pushed her again, quoting a Canadian gynecologist who said that "using smoke and mirrors to say things that make

you happy make you healthier is not fair." He said it suggested Goop products are in the "area of pseudoscience."
Her response:

> We disagree with that whole-heartedly. We really believe that there are healing modalities that have existed for thousands of years, and they challenge maybe a very conventional Western doctor that might not believe, necessarily, in the healing powers of essential oils, or any variety of acupuncture, things that have been tried and tested for hundreds of years. And we find that they are very helpful to people, and that there's an incredible power in the human body to heal itself. I think any time you're trying to move the needle, trying to empower women, you find resistance, and so I think it's just part of what we do.

What Paltrow is doing is not empowering women. It's taking advantage of them. You can't cloak pseudoscience in pseudo-feminism. But at least that last response hit the nail on the head as to why Goop will never be a company that values science over sales. Paltrow readily admits she believes "essential oils" have "healing powers," which has never been demonstrated by *any* peer-reviewed scientific evidence.

If those products masqueraded as actual medicine, they would be illegal. No science team will fix that. And no interview will change the fact that Goop continues selling sham products, many of which are nothing more than expensive placebos.

That being said, Goop isn't the *cause* of why we're here; it's merely a symptom. So, how *did* we get into this mess?

7 Where Did We Go Wrong?

"Those who do not learn history are doomed to repeat it."
—George Santayana, philosopher

In basically any situation, in order to find an appropriate solution, it can help to better understand the problem itself. In this case, we must look at the status and trajectory of modern journalism when asking the question, *"Where did we go wrong?"*

There are many answers to this question, and I won't pretend to know every one of them. I do, however, know that journalism is supposed to speak truth to power. And anything that takes away from that mighty goal, namely holding those in power responsible for their actions, is necessarily bad for journalism. In honor of that smart kid who debated me at the LA Times Festival of Books, I'd like to describe some of the current problems with the current journalistic landscape as well as what caused them.

Clickbait Culture

Part of the problem with the existing news media is that we, as a culture, have become obsessed with "clicks" and largely indifferent toward the quality of the content. Contrary to popular belief, this isn't something that journalists caused, and it isn't something we should be fighting. In fact, I would argue that it's the inevitable result of a society with our advanced technology. We are an intelligent species, but we are also a species that desires instant gratification. As information online becomes more readily available, our brains start to crave it even more. It's natural that we would want to fill our gaps in knowledge, and that we would seek shortcuts to do so, but that impulse has led to a rise in fake and low-quality news stories.

If you've ever read a "headline" that began, "SHOCKING: YOU WON'T BELIEVE . . ." or "YOU NEED TO KNOW THESE THREE THINGS . . ." then you are familiar with what *clickbait* is. It is an attempt to draw views using enticing hooks, and it wouldn't exist if it weren't for the system on which our websites work. The simplest way to monetize a news site is through *advertising,* and the best way to attract advertisers is by having a lot of visitors to the site. Advertisers are willing to pay per page view or even more per click because each click means an ad has been engaged with, which in turn leads to better exposure, higher sales, and greater revenue for the advertiser.

Clickbait is incredibly popular today because, to put it simply, it *works.* Sites make money by posting and promoting articles that are essentially devoid of substantive content. But *why* does it work? One possible reason is that most people don't actually *read* the news. Instead, they read the headline and determine from there whether it's worth sharing. This has been confirmed by a significant amount of research.

One study looking into this found that a majority (59 percent) of links shared on Twitter are never clicked, showing that a lot of news is circulating without review (Gabielkov, Ramachandran, Chaintreau, & Legout, 2016). That confirmed something we saw when a satirical news site published a block of Latin text under the guise of a study on headlines and science, according to the *Washington Post* (Dewey, 2016). "Nearly 46,000 people shared the post, some of them quite earnestly—an inadvertent example, perhaps, of life imitating comedy," a Post reporter wrote.

The content was gibberish but the headline—"Study: 70% of Facebook Users Only Read the Headline of Science Stories before Commenting"—was quite popular, showing that we often judge news based on the headline or the media outlet, or even the credibility of the person who shared the article. But the only way we can truly understand what's going on is if we take the time to read the piece for ourselves.

I'm not saying you have to read every article you see. But if you're going to share an article and increase its influence, it may be worth checking it first.

Consequences of Clickbait

We all know about the online giants that rake in millions via pop-ups, but the clickbait culture has expanded to realms beyond that by impacting *local papers*. For instance, *Forbes* (Helman, 2013) profiled a "local newspaper chain that's actually making good money" in January 2013. The paper is called *Impact*, and it was started by a man named John Garrett. It makes tens of millions of dollars per year while other papers fail. What's the paper's secret? Tons of ads. The *Forbes* article says:

> It doesn't take a lot of personnel to put out a monthly, especially when half its content is ads and coupons. Each edition

usually has one editor and one reporter, plus a general manager, a couple of account executives and a graphic designer. No big-name columnists, no newspaper union members and no pension funds to worry about. . . . Impact has taken a few hits from critics as providing little more than a shopper.

I know some of you are thinking, "So what? It's just advertising. It doesn't affect the quality of the reporting." Well, I beg to differ, my nonexistent antagonist. The *Forbes* piece continues:

Rob Sides, owner of Toy Time, places about 80% of his ad dollars with Impact's Pflugerville-Round Rock edition in order to reach the 90,000 homes in the area. "There's no better deal out there for the return I get," says Sides, who was pleasantly surprised this year when an Impact reporter called to write a feature on his business.

Garrett doesn't scruple publishing nice articles about his accounts. Ken Moncebaiz, who operates K&M Steam Cleaning in Austin, bought an ad in the first issue of Impact and has bought the inside back cover of the paper ever since, shelling out $11,000 a month. He has been rewarded with the occasional story.

. . . .

"One of the most difficult things to explain to our advertisers is when we do a business profile of one of their competitors," says Garrett. "Those are hard but important conversations for the integrity of our product."

Forbes touts *Impact* as a successful local paper, but any paper that provides stories in exchange for advertising revenue is by definition unsuccessful in terms of journalistic merits, in my opinion. If this is the direction of the news industry, we are in big trouble.

Growing Antiscience Sentiment

Part of the increase in fake news, clickbait, and irresponsible citizen reporting can be traced to something beyond journalism: antiscience beliefs running rampant. The content is just responding to the public's demands, which happen to be trending away from science. The rise in antivaccination beliefs leading to global measles outbreaks is just one example of this unfortunate trend. Another example is the Flat Earther movement, which is reportedly growing in numbers and is made up of people who are surprisingly quite serious about their beliefs (McIntyre, 2019).

The antiscience trend can also be seen in the space of genetically modified organisms, where public opposition to the science itself is impossibly high despite demonstrable evidence all but proving its safety and efficacy. In one 2019 study published in *Nature Human Behaviour*, not only did 90 percent of the respondents oppose the use of GMOs, but those who were most against it actually believed they were the most knowledgeable on the subject (despite rating lowest on tests of scientific knowledge) (Fernbach, Light, Scott, Inbar, & Rozin, 2019). Similar results have been seen in vaccine studies (Carroll, 2019) and can be at least partly explained by the *Dunning-Kruger effect*, a cognitive bias in which people overestimate their own abilities because of their distinct lack of expertise on the subject. Perhaps it is this unearned sense of confidence that is leading so many down the antiscience rabbit hole.

Increasing distrust of science and its institutions means that verifiable facts are called into question, and fake news thrives in that unique environment. But there are a number of other factors that contribute to the problem.

In a comical twist, news media itself may be partly responsible for some of the general public's misunderstanding (and therefore, I would argue, its distrust) of scientists and of science in general. Cristine Russell, freelance science writer and president of the Council for the Advancement of Science Writing, says science journalism is suffering due to a combination of factors, including reduced reporter staffing and increasingly complex science issues. Her research indicates that several things could improve the current drought in quality science news, including a downpour of science writer training and communications training for scientists themselves (Russell, 2010):

> Media coverage of controversial scientific issues needs to be improved on both the science and policy sides. Ultimately, better, more balanced coverage of science and technology policy will help the public, and their representatives, understand the crucial issues that individuals, local communities, the United States, and countries of the world face in the years to come.

Science journalists are also being pushed by their audiences to abandon the perch of industry watchdog and instead act as a cheerleader, according to journalist and author Brooke Borel. Borel, who wrote about conflicts of interest that allegedly went undisclosed by science communicator and GMO researcher Kevin Folta, said this is a long-running debate beginning with the origins of science journalism itself:

> Science journalists may write about science, but it's also our job to look beyond wonders, hypotheses and data. It is to look at the people doing the science and whether they have conflicts of interest, or trace where their money is coming from. It is to look at power structures, to see who is included in the work and who is excluded or marginalized, whether because of gender or race or any other identity.

If you're a science journalist who *doesn't* pay attention to corruption and other important issues in the field, I'd argue that you're walking on thin ice, ethically speaking.

Journalism and Ethical Dilemmas

Journalists often run into problems when they don't follow ethical prescriptions. For instance, writers have a responsibility to not only report the facts, but also to protect their sources. Sometimes this includes shielding them from threats to their anonymity, but it can also include guarding their words from being altered in any substantial way by editors or other powers. They must also be careful to avoid plagiarism, libel, and a host of other issues. Basically, it's a lot of responsibility, and not all mainstream journalists take that seriously.

Take Jayson Blair, for example. He was a rising star at the *New York Times* until it was discovered that he had fabricated material for certain news reports. According to the Society of Professional Journalists (Uribarri, n.d.), the paper's reputation—and journalism in general—suffered the devastating consequences in the court of public opinion:

> Jayson Blair advanced quickly during his tenure at *The New York Times*, where he was hired as a full-time staff writer after his internship there and others at *The Boston Globe* and *The Washington Post*. Even accusations of inaccuracy and a series of corrections to his reports on Washington, D.C.-area sniper attacks did not stop Blair from moving on to national coverage of the war in Iraq. But when suspicions arose over his reports on military families, an internal review found that he was fabricating material and communicating with editors from his Brooklyn apartment—or within the *Times* building—rather than from outside New York.

The findings of a 25-member committee headed by Allan Siegal, an assistant managing editor, led to the appointment of a public editor and stricter editorial policies. But staffing changes and higher standards could not change what happened: The *Times*'s reputation was deeply tarnished. Raines and Managing Editor Gerald Boyd resigned in a cloud of mismanagement. Journalism, in general, suffered perhaps the biggest blow to its credibility in U.S. history.

This is a terrible story, and there are many more like it, but the fact is that cases like this are relatively rare because people are usually caught before something like this can occur. That's what editors are for. Here, we have a group of people who ignored red flags and caused a scandal as a result. It certainly caused a lot of problems for journalists, because people were more likely to believe they were all making up stories, but is that a fair assumption?

For the most part, no, we can't blame journalism for this particular journalist's radical behavior—nor for the inappropriate acts of others. What we can do, though, is understand that a major news institution like the *New York Times* should have caught this guy earlier. We can also look at how the industry should address the important issues that rose to the surface thanks to this case. If we're going to restore the public's confidence in journalism, we have to make sure that people like Blair don't succeed in the news industry.

Equal Time

There's another more common instance of ethics affecting the quality of our news. In this case, though, we see how strictly *adhering* to an ethical code can also go wrong. I'm talking about *equal time*.

The Society of Professional Journalists encourages all reporters to be thorough and "support the open and civil exchange of views, even views they find repugnant." This fact, combined with the desire by many journalists to remain completely impartial, has led to something called *false balance*. Dr. David Robert Grimes, a physicist and cancer researcher at Oxford University, has warned of the inevitable danger of this (Grimes, 2016):

> Impartiality lies at the very heart of good journalism—avoiding bias is something on which respectable media outlets pride themselves. This is laudable, as robust debate is vital for a healthy media and, by extension, an informed society. But when the weight of scientific evidence points incontrovertibly one direction, doggedly reporting both "sides" equally can result in misleading coverage.

Dr. Grimes goes on to highlight a report in 2011, which found that the BBC provided too much airtime to "marginal opinions" on the issue of man-made climate change. The report found that the BBC fell victim to an "over-rigid application of editorial guidelines on impartiality." Grimes wrote:

> This situation, known as false balance, arises when journalists present opposing view-points as being more equal than the evidence allows. But when the evidence for a position is virtually incontrovertible, it is profoundly mistaken to treat a conflicting view as equal and opposite by default. With respect to man made climate change, the BBC is far from the only outlet skewing their coverage in the name of balance, and global coverage on climate science remains exceptionally off-kilter with the scientific consensus.

This analysis is reinforced by journalist Bill Moyers, who received thirty-seven Emmys over the course of his career. Quoting legendary environmentalist David Attenborough, who said climate change could mean the "collapse of our civilizations and extinction of much of the natural world," Moyers suggested journalists should cover the issue like Edward R. Murrow covered the start of the Second World War (Moyers, 2019).

Unfortunately, that is not happening. So, while journalism is *not* the enemy of the people, it appears that it most certainly is an arch nemesis to itself. Thankfully, Jonathan Foster, retired University of Sheffield journalism lecturer, has a maxim that could solve the issue entirely:

> If someone says it's raining and another person says it's dry, it's not your job to quote them both. Your job is to look out of the fucking window and find out which is true.

I couldn't agree more.

8 Who Can We Trust?

"Whenever people are well-informed, they can be trusted with their own government."

—Thomas Jefferson, U.S. president

Trust is one of the most important aspects of any relationship, and the one between readers and news providers is no different. When this trust is broken, through a misreported story or a reporter with an agenda or some other journalistic violation, it can be tough—yet not impossible—to fully restore. But just like a good romantic relationship, this type of trust is a two-way street.

Knowing which sources to trust and distrust is probably one of the most important parts of fighting fake news, but making those classifications isn't simple. In fact, I'd argue that in most cases, it's incredibly complex. First of all, the category options are less like "trust" and "distrust" and more like:

- **News sources that generally provide correct information**: Characterized by a consistent record of accuracy, advanced fact-checking process, reporters with training in plagiarism, libel, etc., and editors with experience in the industry. Multiple sets of eyes usually see most stories prior to publication.

- **Websites that often exaggerate or lie in the retelling of events, or make stories up entirely**: Characterized by sloppy reporting, a lack of proper sourcing, "reporters" without any training in journalism, and attention-grabbing headlines. These outlets are often a one-person operation.[11]

You might think of harmful fake news as coming from malicious sites that focus on false information, but the fact is that most of it comes from everyday sites you wouldn't expect. That's not because there aren't bad actors out there who only want to create propaganda, but because those people know the best way to do that involves at least some truthful reporting.

If you're wondering what I mean by that, then think about it from a psychological perspective. Assuming you want to mislead the largest number of people, would it make more sense to spread *only* lies, or to publish a number of claims ranging from true to mostly false? Believe it or not, it always helps a lie to sprinkle in at least a grain of truth.

To prove this point, consider Infowars.com, the website created by Alex Jones to spread his ideas. Alex Jones is known for his false claims, including his suggestion that the government is using chemicals to turn people (and frogs) gay (Lee, 2018). Contrary to what you might assume, the Infowars website looks like most popular news pages. "Featured stories" on November

---

11. And even these two categories aren't enough, because there are several exceptions and news outlets that don't neatly fit into either box.

3, 2019, to pick an arbitrary day, included one about Senator Bernie Sanders saying his ideas are "not far left," as well as one about former vice president Joe Biden confusing Ohio for Iowa. Both of these stories are factual. It's only once you peel back the layers of "normal looking" content that you get to the far-fetched theories Jones has become so famous for.

So, it isn't as easy to identify fake news sources as it would be in an ideal world. Naturally, we want to classify things and put them into specific baskets. It would be nice if I could say, "Anything from [insert site here] is untrustworthy because of conflicts of interest," or, "Don't believe anything [insert person here] says because they are known for false claims." Unfortunately, that's not how the world works because there can and will be exceptions.

This works both ways, though. Just like misinformation-based sites can provide correct information, even the best journalists in the world make mistakes at times. That would make it irresponsible to say you can trust absolutely anything a particular individual says, just like it would be wrong to say a particular site *can't* report something true.

All that said, the *source* of the information isn't usually the most important question. After all, if you are doing your job as an informed participant in society—and fact-checking the articles and books you read—it doesn't really matter where the information originated. We should ultimately judge all ideas based on their merits, and not by who happened to have uttered them last.

As a scientific skeptic, I definitely know the importance of *doubt*. I think keeping in mind that certain "news" sources aren't reliable is of the utmost importance. That being said, it would be a logical fallacy to completely discount a confirmed fact solely *because* of its source. So, what do you do? For me, it's pretty simple. I listen to what I'm told with a critical ear, no matter the source, and never believe what I hear just because it was shared online or communicated on a news channel.

Now, am I saying that sources never matter? Certainly not. If you are considering whether something is true, it may be important to evaluate the source and consider its record. If, however, you know something is true (or it is confirmed by other, more reputable sources), and you discount it *because* of its source, that is a basic reasoning failure. So, evaluation of the source is definitely important. But that can't be the beginning and end of the process. From there, you must *analyze* the information itself to see if the report makes sense in context. This is how I approach what I read and hear.

A Newsroom

If you acknowledge that the source isn't *everything* but still want to take it into consideration, there are a variety of factors you should pay attention to. For one, is this a real news agency or just an individual with an agenda? I will be the first to tell you that *some* productions that refer to themselves as "news" are merely advertisers—or even political avatars—playing a complicated shell game. I have long criticized purported news platforms that promote their own political beliefs at the expense of the facts, give unwarranted attention to those promoting dangerous medical theories, or don't follow journalistic ethics.

So I'm *not* saying you should implicitly trust anything labeled "news" or distrust anything not vetted by some corporation (I myself have broken stories without an official newsroom structure). That way of thinking about news is always a recipe for disaster. What I *am* saying, however, is that agencies that have the proper safeguards in place shouldn't be immediately written off. In those cases, it's important to remember that a newsroom at very least often guarantees that multiple sets of eyes saw and approved the content. Still, there are a number of exceptions to this guideline. After all, I can think of individual reporters I'd trust any day over certain "news" organizations.

The Reporter's Record and Training

Regardless of the news agency, it's also important to look at the reporter(s) whose byline appears on the specific piece you're reading. On most reputable sites, you should be able to click their name and read a bio, which will in turn usually have social media links. Does that person have a strong record of quality articles? Has that person worked for a company or organization that would provide journalism training, including practice on how to avoid libel, plagiarism, and allegations of bias? How long have they been writing professionally? How many corrections and clarifications has the reporter had to make in the last year? If their organization doesn't *do* corrections, that's a red flag all by itself.

No reporter is perfect, so seeing a correction on their record doesn't necessarily mean anything at all. Even a series of corrections might not be a red flag for a seasoned reporter who takes time to update their stories when they are in need. It's less about whether they've made mistakes, and more about the *type* of mistakes and how they have acted in response to being confronted with their errors. Were the corrections substantive ones? Do they graciously thank the person correcting them, and then go on to update the piece? Do they make an effort to spread word of the correction, taking into consideration that retractions and amendments rarely receive the same level of attention online and in other media? Do they fact-check their work *before* actually publishing their story in order to prevent corrections? Do they contact relevant parties in a particular case? These are all important questions, especially when they're taken into consideration together, as each on their own won't tell you very much.

Simply noticing a mistake a reporter has made may not tell you anything at all, but seeing a pattern of changing the facts to suit a narrative does, and that's something to look out for. In other words, it's more about the *attitude* than the errors. Here are some questions to ask yourself on that front:

1. Are the reporter's stories generally balanced, with quotes and perspectives from different sides?

2. Do they violate ethical guidelines, such as by accepting expensive gifts from their sources?

3. Do they give proper credit when taking info from others?

These are just some of the questions you should be asking and, just like before, they are best used together and not individually. Training is another key component of the reporter-reader trust connection. If the journalist isn't properly trained, they *could* be doing harm overall even if they have the best of intentions.

A trustworthy writer will have, for instance, a comprehensive understanding of libel, plagiarism, free speech, and other issues that are important to reporting the news. This understanding must go beyond a dictionary definition. In addition to knowing these key words and how to avoid being caught on the wrong side of their implications, a quality reporter will also have been trained on precedence and case law on the issues they can run up against. They should also get regular updates on litigation involving their fellow reporters, and workshops from attorneys with lots of experience on speech issues.

Trusted and Untrusted Sources

One of the most common questions I get is something along the lines of, "Can you provide me with a list of trusted sources for news?" And as much as I love the spirit of the question—it shows that the individual is interested in facts and doesn't want a source that will deceive them regularly—it's always a difficult one because no source is going to be 100 percent accurate or beyond reproach when it comes to questioning. In fact, any news agency worth its salt would encourage its readers to question everything, including what it has published. In many ways, it would be easier to make a list of individuals and organizations *not* to trust, but even that would be a logical fallacy. You have to check sources preliminarily, but ultimately, it's up to you to research the content.

Still, it doesn't hurt to provide some of my favorite sources for news, which tend to provide a relatively unbiased look at what's really happening in the world. Nor does it do any real harm to give a heads up on specific news sources with documented abuses and issues.[12]

News Sources That Generally Provide Accurate Information

- **ABC News.** While most rating sites say ABC News generally leans to the left in its political analysis, it remains one of the most credible outlets. That's not to say, however, that it doesn't make mistakes. In October 2019, for instance, ABC posted a video that was wrongly identified as showing "Turkey's military bombing Kurd civilians." It ultimately pulled the video after it was debunked, but experts warned not to

---

12. These lists are by no means exhaustive. In fact, both lists represent a minimalist effort just to show the kinds of things to look for when reviewing news sites' credibility.

let occasional lapses in standards ruin trust in the news (Adams, 2019).

- **Associated Press.** The Associated Press is generally considered one of the most reliable, and least biased, news agencies, and it has been for many years. That being said, its writers—like all human beings—do make mistakes. Still, their mistakes are usually relatively minor and there's almost always a good-faith effort from the writers to get the story right. Many of their errors relate to misspellings, or to failing to uphold the agency's own editorial policies on issues related to gender (Dye, 2019). More importantly than its specific errors, though, is the fact that AP has a transparent system for reporting and responding to corrections and clarifications. On its correctives page, AP states:

  > When we're wrong, we must say so as soon as possible. When we make a correction in the current cycle, we point out the error and its fix in the editor's note. A correction must always be labeled a correction in the editor's note.

- **National Public Radio.** Like the Associated Press, NPR has a substantial accuracy plank in its editorial ethics handbook. Like most news networks, however, it has made serious errors—such as erroneously reporting that Rep. Gabby Giffords (D-AZ) was killed during a shooting in Arizona, when she had actually been seriously injured. Instead of hiding those mistakes, NPR highlights a few of them as "case studies" on its accuracy site so that they can serve as tools for reporter education. Among other things, NPR says it erred in not bringing in senior editors onto the Giffords story before the broadcast.

- **Reuters.** Reuters uses its articles to link to the company's standards and "trust principles" for preserving "independence, integrity, and freedom from bias in the gathering and dissemination of information and news." It is considered to be one of the least biased credible news sites, yet it, too, makes some mistakes. In fact, the Committee for Accuracy in Middle East Reporting and Analysis keeps a list of Reuters media corrections prompted by the organization, with an emphasis on articles relating to Israeli issues.

- **Wall Street Journal.** The *Wall Street Journal* is an example of a news organization that tends to score high on credibility while leaning right in some of its political analyses. The newspaper has a solid reputation among readers, but it, too, has had its share of correction scandals. In 2012, for instance, it was criticized for "numerous, uncorrected mistakes" on the paper's editorial pages (Edmonson, 2012).

Websites That Often Exaggerate or Lie, or Make Stories Up Entirely

- **Addicting Info.** Addicting Info isn't a concrete "fake news" site in that it doesn't perpetuate knowingly and blatantly false information, but it does have a strong political bias, which, combined with its lack of journalistic checks and balances, causes exaggerated or false stories to be published fairly regularly. The website was listed as a "clickbait and hoax" source by Sewanee University's Jessie Ball duPont Library (Fake News, 2019). Ironically, Addicting Info's Facebook page banner says, "Believing Fox News is like believing The Onion," referencing a known satire site.

- **Bipartisan Report.** Bipartisan Report, another popular site that has been given the "clickbait and hoax" designation by Sewanee, is anything but "bipartisan" in its delivery of heavily exaggerated information for credulous liberals. While Bipartisan Report founder Justin Brotman doesn't like the site being called "fake news," because it doesn't completely fabricate stories, he admitted he modelled Bipartisan Report after Fox News and that it could reasonably be called Breitbart for the left (Westneat, 2016).

- **ABCNews.com.co.** ABCNews.com.co is not to be confused with ABC News, which uses the site ABCNews.go.com, although its owners would like it if you would make that mistake. In fact, it uses almost the exact same logo and URL as the real thing. Unlike some of the noted clickbait sites, this one seems to knowingly spread misinformation for profit. It relies on its similarities to a credible site to get clicks, and uses a Colombian domain, .co, to avoid United States regulation.

- **Palmer Report.** The Palmer Report is another "news site" that provides skewed content (with a liberal twist) featuring sensational headlines and stories with unverified conspiracy theories. Run by Bill Palmer, the report casts itself as a news site but doesn't have any of the necessary factors to ensure veracity. Brooke Binkowski, formerly the managing editor for Snopes, said it is "very harmful" (Meyer, 2017).

- **NewsPunch.** NewsPunch, a fake news site with a far-right political bias, has been widely recognized as a fake news site since it went by another name, YourNewsWire.com. NewsPunch, in an apparent attempt to distract from its status as an unreliable source of news, has even gone as far as to publish a story saying the concerns about "fake news" are vastly overstated (Adl-Tabatabai, 2016).

- **Infowars.** Infowars is probably the most well-known site on Sewanee's "clickbait and hoax" list. Run by Alex Jones, Infowars is known for perpetuating far-right conspiracy theories, including saying the deadly Sandy Hook shooting was a hoax. It was listed as a fake news site to "watch out" for by CBS News (CBS News, n.d.).

- **Natural News.** Natural News is a widely recognized health conspiracy theory and fake news site run by a man named Mike Adams (aka "The Health Ranger"). This is one of the most dangerous types of fake news websites because it presents medical misinformation, including false reports linking vaccines to autism, on which some people will decide to base their treatment.

It's important to point out that there are also many sites that fit into a middle ground between the two categories above. Normally, these are news sites that have generally good reporting, but also a political bias that tends to lead to some unintentional exaggerations or even inaccuracies.

Become Someone Others Can Trust

Learning the ins and outs of quality journalism, as well as its ethical norms, common pitfalls, and standard operating procedures, can help readers learn who they can trust and who they probably *shouldn't*. But it can perform another function, too. Namely, it can make the reader themselves more informed, and therefore more trustworthy as a participant in our advanced society.

We talked at the beginning of this chapter about how the trust between readers and reporters must go both ways, and it's an important point that shouldn't be passed over. What I mean by this "two-way street" concept is that consumers of content must act in good faith just as much as the reporter. Just as it is the writer's responsibility not to mislead or misconstrue facts, it is the reader's task to listen with an open mind—without intentionally misrepresenting the reporting or data they see. It's also the reader's job to take more than a cursory look at what they're consuming, and make sure it's not the work of bad actors who imitate real journalists.

By being educated on the processes of journalism and paying closer attention to what we read, we can become knowledgeable members of the general population, and are in a better place to advocate for the changes that we deem necessary. And by only sharing the highest-quality content, it's possible to *become* the solid information source we all seek, and help friends and loved ones find their way, too.

The first step to getting there is becoming well informed.

9 Fake News, Real Damage

"As long as anger, paranoia and misinformation drive our political debate, there are unhinged souls among us who will feel justified in turning to violent remedies for imagined threats."

—David Horsey, editorial cartoonist

A lot of people think fake news is harmless, or that it causes minimal damage that can be ignored because (A) the people who fall for it "deserve it" or (B) it is not worth jeopardizing free speech to regulate the news market.

First, let's address the claim that those who believe a fake news story deserve whatever they get as a result. This mindset is inherently based on victim-blaming, and has no basis in reality. We know that's the case because *everyone* has fallen for *some* piece of misinformation. Whether it was a conspiracy-ridden website with tons of red flags, or an urban myth passed to you by oral tradition, *even you* have been fooled in this way before.[13]

---

13. None of this even touches on the fact that those who *believe* fake news

It's easy to write someone off for being "stupid" if they believe something false, but that sense of superiority itself is false (and pretty hypocritical). If you do this, you likely aren't taking into consideration a variety of factors, including poverty, education availability, and susceptibility to indoctrination at the time. For instance, consider criminal "psychic" fraudsters, who often rip people off for millions of dollars when they're more vulnerable than they have ever been in their lives: when they are grieving for a loved one. This type of fraud is really no different than, say, a white-collar Ponzi scheme, yet often observers think the victims of psychic scammers somehow deserved it while the Ponzi investors are generally thought to deserve restitution.

Next, we should talk about the 800-pound gorilla in the room: free speech. Before we can do so, however, we must *define* free speech and explain its many limitations.

Contrary to popular belief, free speech is *not* an American concept that exists only in the United States. Several countries have what could be called freedom of speech to varying degrees, with some nations having extremely strict limitations on certain communications. That being said, I live in the United States, so I'll start with *our* definition based on the First Amendment of the Constitution.

Freedom of Speech [free-duh m uhv speech]
noun phrase

1. The legal right to express one's opinions freely. (Merriam-Webster, n.d.)

2. The right of people to express their opinions publicly without governmental interference, subject to the laws against

---

items aren't necessarily the only ones who suffer.

libel, incitement to violence or rebellion, etc. (Dictionary.
com, n.d.)

Example sentence: The man who posted incendiary things on
social media was protected from prosecution by freedom of
speech, but he was not safe from being fired by his employer.

Under these definitions of freedom of speech, we can see that
the term is *not* used to guarantee the right to say anything you
want. Instead, it protects citizens from being *prosecuted* for their
words. All citizens are still subject to *other* consequences, including social and employment pressures.

Those who believe in *unlimited* free speech don't understand
or accept the existing limitations to speech, but they are actually
there for good reasons. For instance, if you incite actions that
would harm others, that's not considered protected free speech.
It also doesn't include the right to distribute obscene materials,
or to burn draft cards as an antiwar protest, according to the
U.S. court system (United States Courts, n.d.).

Freedom of speech also doesn't apply to private platforms,
such as social media sites and other peoples' businesses and
homes. In other words, you can't simply say whatever you want
without repercussions from *any* private parties. The protections
free speech *does* provide apply only to government intervention, so other entities can still impose basically whatever limits
they want. This comes up most when people allege free speech
violations against social media sites when they are banned or
temporarily suspended for violating the company's terms and
conditions.

As someone who has been banned from social media more
than a dozen times for violating terms, including instances when
I did *nothing* that could come close to a violation, I can assure
you this is not a problem with our free speech. For example, I
once received a *death threat* that I reported to the correspond-

ing social media platform. I was informed that the attack, in which a person said they would chop off my head and included a screenshot from a search showing the address to my house where my family and I live, did *not* violate the company's stated policies.

I decided to post the threat publicly, along with my story of reporting it without any success, and I was banned from the platform for thirty days.

Again, this is not an issue with freedom of speech in the United States. You could argue that it's a problem with social media companies and their process for reporting and enforcement, but it's impossible to make this a constitutional issue. And the same goes for everyone else who is banned or suspended from social media as well.

While I may not agree with *every* exemption to the U.S. free speech system, I do think it's necessary to *have* exceptions. And I think most rational people, if confronted with the evidence, would accept that fact.

So, keeping in mind that definition of free speech, it is entirely possible to battle fake news through enforcement of our current laws along with significant corporate and individual cooperation on the issue. It's also possible for the government to intervene to stop fake news if it reaches a level of inciting violence.

The question then becomes: where do we draw the line between free speech and fake news that endangers lives?

Fatal Fake News

If you think fake news is all about clicks and that it can't possibly cause real damage, consider the story of Ricardo Flores, a young man who was studying to become a lawyer and earn money for his family. He was in the town of Acatlán in Puebla,

Mexico, where he was visiting family, when he and his uncle were rushed by a mob, beaten, and set on fire (Martínez, 2018). All of this happened because of a rumor that spread via WhatsApp, a Facebook-owned texting service, without any obvious monetary motive. Ricardo and his uncle were brutally murdered based on false claims linking them to another unverified story involving child kidnapping and organ harvesting. In other words, fake news literally killed these two innocent men. This isn't the first mob-related death in the area, but the issue may be worsening thanks to the problem of fake news, the *Los Angeles Times* reports (McDonnell & Sanchez, 2018):

> The barbaric episode—reminiscent of mob killings in India fueled by viral messages—illustrates how in an era of proliferating smartphone use, rumors looped on social media and messaging platforms such as WhatsApp can generate hysteria and vigilante justice.
>
> Mob attacks are nothing new in Mexico, where rampant crime, ineffective policing and a pervasive sense that lawbreakers go unpunished fuel citizen outrage. Cellphone video of townsfolk pummeling cornered suspects accused of robberies and other misdeeds is a regular feature on TV news.
>
> . . . .
>
> Law enforcement officials fear that hoaxes spread on Facebook, WhatsApp and other platforms may be exacerbating the disturbing trend.

This mob killing based on fake news may seem like a one-off incident that doesn't require any further investigation, but the fact is it is part of a much larger pattern. In fact, this type of thing happens pretty regularly in India, and WhatsApp often finds itself in those headlines, too.

In 2018, for example, five men were killed by a mob who

had heard on the messaging system that there were bands of kidnappers around. Just as was the case in Mexico, some versions of the rumor included allegations of organ harvesting (McLaughlin, 2018).

Amid Hong Kong residents' protests against mainland China, we saw similar instances of misinformation motivating violence and putting lives at risk. Faulty rumors inundated both sides of the dispute, resulting in someone being shot in November 2019, according to Bloomberg News (Banjo & Lung, 2019):

> As Hong Kong's anti-government protests stretch into their 23rd straight week, the city is being inundated with online rumors, fake news and propaganda from both sides of the political divide. The polarizing rhetoric is fueling distrust and violence, making it harder to resolve the crisis that has plunged Hong Kong into a recession and raised doubts about the city's role as Asia's premier financial hub.
>
> "False information feeds itself to polarize public opinion," said Masato Kajimoto, an assistant professor at Hong Kong University's Journalism and Media Studies Centre, who has spent the last seven years studying fake news. "I worry that it reaches a point where reconciliation of this divide is no longer possible."

Another instance of blowback from misinformation didn't result in any deaths, but *did* include the firing of a rifle in public, and things could have been much worse if the situation had played out differently. I'm talking about the infamous Pizzagate conspiracy theory that spread like wildfire in far-right circles. If you haven't heard of it before, the general premise of the claim is that there was a pedophile ring being run by top Democrat politicians like Hillary Clinton, using a Washington, DC pizza place as a front. One man, twenty-eight-year-old Edgar M.

Welch, read the false information online and drove six hours to see for himself. He ultimately fired his AR-15, but no one was hurt and he was arrested on site (Kang & Goldman, 2016).

Of course, vigilante "justice" attacks aren't the only ways for fake news to cause serious harm.

Medical Misinformation

In the medical field, the problem of fake news regularly kills people. In fact, "medical misinformation is already having adverse effects on global health," according to one study looking into false claims related to health (Armstrong & Naylor, 2019):

> It requires a robust and coordinated response from health professionals, organizations, institutions, and mainstream media. Medical journals now have an opportunity to galvanize and support this important effort.

That same study found that, while medical misinformation is nothing new, the "online world facilitates direct-to-consumer marketing by phony experts, celebrities with armies of Twitter followers, and legions of independent digital scammers, including some physicians." The researchers wrote:

> The result has been torrents of misinformation on topics as varied as the safety and effectiveness of vaccinations, the Zika virus outbreak, water fluoridation, genetically modified foods, and treatments for common diseases. For those disadvantaged, despairing, and understandably distrustful of government, these "alternative truths" align with shared skepticism about scientific medicine and belief in traditional remedies.

I spoke with Dr. David Robert Grimes, a physicist and cancer researcher at the University of Oxford, about the many potential problems misinformation poses to the medical field. He pointed out that, while it is a problem in every field, its harm is most evident in the sphere of medicine. In an interview, Dr. Grimes told me:

> Health is an issue of fundamental importance, and yet information about it online especially has been utterly dominated by falsehoods, perpetuated by charlatans and fools. The consequences of this are staggering—we're seeing a dark renaissance of once nigh-on conquered diseases like measles, driven by antivaccine propaganda. We're also seeing people with chronic illnesses being hawked all manner of dangerous pseudoscience, especially at people with cancer. Patients who subscribe to these modalities tend to delay or defer conventional effective treatment, and this has a marked negative impact on survival.

Dr. Grimes explained exactly how and why medical myths have permeated every facet of society for all of recorded history:

> Since as long as people have gotten ill, there has been purveyors of snake-oil eager to profiteer off misery. And oddly, this doesn't seem to correlate with wealth or education; pseudosciences like homeopathy and reiki are subscribed to mainly by middle-class, affluent people. Similarly, antivaccine sentiment is frequently strongest in affluent areas. Partially this is born of a misguided idea that things that are "natural" are superior to the "synthetic," but this is utterly misguided. Natural is such an evanescent adjective as to be useless; arsenic and Ebola are natural, but one would be ill-advised to sprinkle them on their breakfast cereal.

We also talked about how vulnerable people are most often affected by misinformation on medical matters:

> The problem is that, ultimately, vulnerable people are the most harmed by falsehoods. If a relatively healthy person with a minor ailment falls for pseudoscience, in general this mistake will not be life-threatening. However, if a person with a serious illness falls under the sway of charlatans or fools, the consequences are frequently tragic. In this respect, those with chronic or life-threatening conditions are a group far more vulnerable to the toxic influence of falsehood.

This is, unfortunately, absolutely true. Far too often vulnerable communities are affected by misinformation, including some that directly targets them, and the results are horrific. Fortunately, it's never too late to combat obviously dangerous misinformation.

Switching Sides

For a specific example of harm caused by vaccine misinformation, we need to look no further than Debbie Roscoe and her daughter, Ellie. Debbie didn't complete Ellie's full course of inoculations when she was a kid for a very specific reason: Andrew Wakefield's notorious (and thoroughly discredited) study falsely linking the measles, mumps, and rubella (MMR) vaccine to autism (This Morning, 2019).

Wakefield's study, which was ultimately retracted, was published in 1998, when Debbie was deciding what to do about her daughter's follow-up round of important vaccinations. She noted that "autism was in the newspaper" following the Wakefield publication, and that facts weren't as immediately available then as they are today with the growth of the internet.

Unfortunately, at the age of twenty-three, Ellie contracted a case of the measles that wasn't properly diagnosed and became life threatening, forcing her mother to acknowledge her error and switch sides in the vaccine debate. After that, Debbie began begging other parents to vaccinate their kids despite the unfounded yet widespread fear campaign.

"The facts were not really available at that time because were going back many moons ago. Now you can get the full facts," Debbie said.

Debbie isn't the only former opponent of vaccination to change their tune after a close call with a loved one. Kristen O'Meara, a Chicago mother of three daughters who opposed childhood vaccines, similarly altered her perception on the important issue. In the case of Kristen, though, all three of her girls became so sick they could have died. "I put my kids at risk. I wish that I had taken more time to research from both sides before my children were born," said Kristen, who became convinced in her antivaccination beliefs after scouring the internet for information on their potential harm (Babich, 2016).

These aren't isolated incidents. Christine Vigeant has a similar story. She was an antivaxxer because her lifestyle and alternative attachment parenting lent itself to such antiscientific health beliefs. She ultimately changed her mind, but not due to skeptics presenting her with the facts. She actually said that made things worse, as she felt like she was being attacked. This is a basic psychological phenomenon—we are built for self-justification—so how do we get around all that?

For Christine, the answer didn't come fast. She said the seed of doubt was planted only after one of her fellow attachment parenters said she had vaccinated her young kids. That led to a conversation between like-minded individuals that eventually caused a change of heart that could possibly save lives (Dastagir, 2019).

Fake News Networks

When I think of fake news causing deaths, the first thing that comes to my mind is something not a lot of people even know about. It's a swarm of underground communities based entirely on false information—the seedy underbelly of the fake news world. Although their propaganda has seeped into conspiracy sites and even mainstream news networks, it is primarily spread through social media. Specifically, closed and secret groups on Facebook are known for enabling these people.

I'm talking about pseudoscientific "medicine" and how certain so-called treatments are actually extremely dangerous. There is a difference between this and placebo-based treatments, which might be indirectly fatal based on denial of modern medicine but do not kill people in themselves (such as petitionary prayer and crystals being used instead of chemotherapy to treat cancer).

These groups are secret for a reason. The purported treatments are not harmless, like a homeopathic drink that has been diluted a billion times until it lacks active ingredients. In many cases, they are *deadly*. For example, you've probably heard of turpentine, a paint thinner and one of the poisons most commonly ingested by children. Well, there are people who drink it to "cure" *literally every disease*. Worse than that is the fact that people also take in turpentine via an enema. And worst of all: people force this on their kids, including those with autism, AIDS, and cancer.

I discovered the turpentine pseudoscience community when a screenshot from a private group went viral among science communicators. The post showed a woman named Stephanie who said she was on the third day of her turpentine and castor oil "protocol" and experiencing "lots of red liquid" during her bowel movements despite not eating anything that color.

"Maybe old and damaged intestine wall is coming out," a turpentine supporter wrote in response to Stephanie's post. "Don't worry."

I was confused and intrigued by this *ingesting turpentine* thing, so I tracked down the group from which the screenshot was taken. I used an alter ego account to make connections to the group and earn an invite. At the time I requested admission, there were more than 640 members in the closed group, called, "Parasites cause all disease—turpentine cure." Once I got in (I wrote, *"I've been sicker than usual lately and I heard this group could help."*), I saw immediately that leaders and members alike promoted consumption of the highly toxic and fatal paint solvent. I saw real people who had been consuming turpentine and experiencing horrible side effects as a result. I saw people sharing stories, seeking support, and hoping to cure everything from scabies to "electromagnetic hypersensitivity" to herpes, and every ailment in between. Keep in mind this isn't medicine; it's turpentine.

Turpentine is made from pine tree sap, so it appeals to the "natural remedy" crowd, but that doesn't mean it is safe. It is actually highly toxic, and can cause vomiting, coma, and irritation of respiratory pathways (Filipsson, 1996).

After the initial shock of joining up, it was mostly just a gruesome waiting game. I sat around in that group and watched person after person complain about horrific symptoms of turpentine, only to be encouraged to continue its use by those who illegally *sell it to them*, all while knowing I couldn't step forward without jeopardizing my position on the inside, which could allow me to help more than one individual. After all, this is just *one* private group I stumbled upon by accident, but there are others out there who do this. And they all need help.

Black Salve

I wrote about my experience RE: turpentine[14] and hoped to simply move on. Unfortunately, I soon learned that these sprawling Facebook groups promoting the ingestion of solvent were just the tip of the proverbial iceberg. Weeks later, I learned about another alternative "medicine" putting cancer patients' lives at risk: black salve.

Black salve treatments are a form of "quackery" first documented in 1955, according to Dr. Grimes:

> While most fake cancer cures are functionally useless, black salve is actively harmful. It is a paste that destroys skin tissue, and is highly dangerous. It is also functionally useless as a cancer treatment. For this reason, it is illegal in many places around the world, but online disinformation has seen trade in it flourish, despite the very real dangers it brings, with dangerous infections and even amputations of afflicted areas not uncommon.

Black salves are sold around the world as a cure for cancer, with fraudsters claiming it draws the bad cells out of the skin. Unfortunately, that's just not the case. Instead, the salve can be extremely corrosive to skin tissues (FDA, 2009).

The Food and Drug Administration's warnings haven't stopped people from treating their cancer with black salve, and it hasn't kept some of them from dying. After joining a group called "BLACK SALVE RESEARCH GROUP," I witnessed just that with a woman named Theresa. She was diagnosed with cancer in early 2017 and, by the end of that year, she was

---

14. McAfee, D. (2017, October 20). *These People Think Drinking Turpentine Will Cure Any Disease*. Retrieved from No Sacred Cows: https://www.patheos.com/blogs/nosacredcows/2017/10/people-are-drinking-turpentine/

applying the topical paste that eats away tissue and rejecting modern medicine.

My introduction to Theresa was on October 31, 2017, when she posted that she had started topical reaction and that the tumor in her breast was "really swollen" due to internal interactions from the black salve. "It is very sensitive to the touch and a tiny bit of pain," Theresa wrote to fellow salvers in the private group. A photo accompanied her text.

After about a month, Theresa posted additional photos of her breast on which she had been using the black salve. By that time, she was already beginning to experience the necrosis that is so common with this type of "treatment." She said she "never thought" it would react that way.

By December of that year, the salve had eaten away more and more of Theresa's breast tissue. She posted graphic photos in the group, and even asked for suggestions, but she ruled out medical intervention. "And please no comments to see a doctor. I've been there," the woman wrote. "This is my path and I trust in it and my God who is healing me."

By January 2018, it appeared as though Theresa had changed her tune regarding turning to medical doctors. She posted on January 27 that her "surgery moved to Monday," and then a month later she was on her way to her "first chemo treatment," which is something she should have done long before that point. Unfortunately, Theresa chose to put off treatment for too long. She passed away in April 2018 after spending time in the hospital for a prolonged infection.

This is a truly tragic story. No one deserves a death like this, especially one that was likely preventable if only the patient had gotten treatment earlier. My only hope is that others will learn from this story, and not repeat Theresa's mistakes. If you are diagnosed with cancer, please get medical help, and don't rely on strangers on Facebook!

Drinking Bleach

It was my investigations into turpentine and black salve that led to yet another dangerous "treatment" risking the lives of thousands of patients. In this case, it's something called "Miracle Mineral Solution." Of course, they call it that because "industrial bleaching agent" doesn't sound as safe.

The *real* name for MMS is chlorine dioxide, and the FDA has been warning against its use since October 2010. The solution "becomes a potent chemical that's used as a bleach when mixed according to package directions," officials said at the time (FDA, 2010):

> FDA has received several reports of consumers who got sick from drinking the MMS and citrus juice mixture. The reports say consumers suffered from nausea, severe vomiting, and life-threatening low blood pressure caused by dehydration.
>
> FDA officials are urging anyone who has had a negative reaction to consult a health care professional as soon as possible.

By 2019, the FDA's warning was more informed, and therefore more dire. In August of that year, the agency said the recommended protocol for mixing the materials results in a "dangerous bleach which has caused serious and potentially life-threatening side effects."

In the most recent warning, FDA acting commissioner Ned Sharpless said:

> Miracle Mineral Solution and similar products are not FDA-approved, and ingesting these products is the same as drinking bleach. Consumers should not use these products, and

parents should not give these products to their children for any reason.

Despite the repeated cautionary statements from regulators, many people have resorted to the bleach product for themselves or their kids. One such individual is Laurel Austin, a Kansas mom who gives MMS to her two autistic adult sons. Laurel says her kids are "vaccine-injured" and claims the protocol has improved one's communication skills. The father of those boys and Laurel's ex-husband, Brad, has been fighting to get a court order preventing the MMS protocol but has so far been unsuccessful.

As one reporter explains for NBC News, the mom's motivations for providing the bleach are based on "fake science" (Zadrozny, 2019):

> The Austins' case illustrates the ways in which online health misinformation can become so pervasive that it begins to sway not only those on the fringe who are seeking alternate treatments and explanations but also authorities, including doctors and the police, who are charged with protecting the most vulnerable.

The reporter mentions the police and doctors because Brad has appealed to both in his attempts to stop the application of the bleach, but to no avail. Laurel is part of an organized MMS network that would make it easy to ensure she always has a doctor's note endorsing the controversial procedure, and police dropped their case upon seeing the medical exemption.

Dr. Grimes has traced the origins of MMS back to Jim Humble, a former Scientologist who now has his own "healing" church (Grimes, 2017). Dr. Grimes said that, while MMS is often marketed for autistic individuals as it was with Brad and

Laurel's kids, it is also pitched to cancer patients and basically anyone else. This, he explained, should be a red flag in itself:

> When a single agent is lauded as having curative power for a wide variety of completely different conditions, this should be considered a glaring siren of potential pseudoscience.

Black salve, MMS, and turpentine are just three examples of dangerous "remedies" that plague the medical community. We have barely even scratched the surface; there are many more! In fact, there is a whole "rogue's gallery of ostensible treatments for cancer" that are both ineffective and actively dangerous, according to Dr. Grimes:

> There are restrictive diets like the alkaline and keto diet that can imperil a patient's life, the ingestion of toxic compounds from bleach to caesium chloride, unsafe exposure to high oxygen and ozone. The FDA list of fake cancer cures, while nonexhaustive, runs to hundreds of items long. But even biologically inert treatments can kill people with cancer, if they cause them to delay or refuse conventional treatment. And sadly, this all too often happens. When it comes to our well-being, there is no safe dose of misinformation.

The fact is that, even if we expose every single fraudulent medical procedure, we won't solve the problem. People will continue to resort to dangerous home remedies like these as long as they distrust the scientific community, which hits at the core of the issue.

To make matters worse, fraudulent cures target the most vulnerable communities, like autistic children and cancer patients of all ages. They take people who need help, or who other people *think* need help, and then make life worse for them by giving them false hopes and adding new health issues.

Often the victims of these "treatments" have no say in the matter and, even when they do, that decision is usually based on false information and motivated by desperation. So the victim almost never has a true, informed choice.

Distracting from Treatment

Even when it isn't one of these dangerous medical treatments at issue, and instead it's a placebo-based treatment the patient is taking, there is still measurable harm. While it doesn't directly cause the damage, it's easy to draw a line between these non-sense treatments and the denial of legitimate medical services, according to Dr. Jen Gunter, an OB/GYN and pain medicine physician (Gunter, 2018):

> So what's the harm of spending money on charcoal for non-existent toxins or vitamins for expensive urine or grounding bedsheets to better connect you with the earth's electrons?
>
> . . . .
>
> Here's what: the placebo effect or "trying something natural" can lead people with serious illnesses to postpone effective medical care. Every doctor I know has more than one story about a patient who died because they chose to try to alkalinize their blood or gambled on intravenous vitamins instead of getting cancer care. Data is emerging that cancer patients who opt for alternative medical practices, many promoted by companies that sell products of questionable value, are more likely to die.

Dr. Grimes pointed out that "all ailments have myths surrounding them," and pointed out that lots of people still believe high-dose vitamin C can cure the common cold. He told me:

This was a myth perpetuated by Nobel laureate Linus Pauling in the 1970s which endures to this day, even though it is absolutely untrue. There is a multitude of similar claims about common ailments, but of course misinformation here rarely has the same awful consequence it does when applied to more serious health conditions.

These nothing "treatments" may not be a *direct* harm, but society would undoubtedly be better off without them.

Deepfakes

One of the biggest risks of fake news stems from something we don't see every day, but that will continue to be a major presence in the future of fake news: deepfake videos. These ultra-realistic clips seem to have unlimited power to negatively impact every facet of our society, including and especially elections that affect all our lives.

Deepfakes have so much power because they can basically show anyone doing anything, whether or not the content is based in reality, and we as humans are visual learners. If humans see it, they tend to also believe it.

As is the case with many new industries bursting onto the scene, deepfake videos are largely being driven not by fake news but by pornography. In fact, one report estimated that about 96 percent of deepfake videos could be considered porn that is "nonconsensual." In other words, people are using existing porn videos to make it appear as though celebrities are in the clip (Winder, 2019).

But that technology can, and likely will, also be used to interfere with legitimate elections. In fact, with the speed at which our video editing technology is improving, it wouldn't surprise me if deepfake videos became the prominent form of political misinformation within a few short years. If a picture is worth a thousand words, a deepfake video could be worth a million misplaced votes for an unworthy politician. Consider the deepfake clip that showed Jeremy Corbyn urging voters to support rival candidate Boris Johnson as prime minister, despite the fact that nothing like that came close to happening (Pettit, 2019). This is already starting to happen.

Deepfakes are "the most powerful false-news weapon in history" and they are soon going to be too convincing for experts to disprove, according to Thomas Kent, president and chief executive of Radio Free Europe/Radio Liberty, which reports the news in twenty-two countries where a free press is either banned by the government or not established (Radio Free Europe/Radio Liberty, n.d.). In a 2018 op-ed published by the *Washington Post*, Kent wrote (Kent, 2018):

> At a political level, deftly constructed video could show a political leader advocating for the reverse of what she stands for, or portray bloody events that never happened. It could trigger riots, swing elections, and sow panic and despair.

He added:

> At a business and personal level, it could be equally dangerous. Fake statements by chief executives or banking officials could throw financial markets into turmoil. False videos could be created about anyone's private life, with devastating effects.

Kent also notes that deepfakes are particularly influential in large part because of the attitudes toward video evidence in our society. He said video has been the "ultimate argument-settler" for years:

Online news outlets routinely hyperlink videos into stories to buttress the credibility of their reporting. Dash-cam video is often the clincher in claims of police malfeasance. Society now has to learn that video no longer guarantees reliability. Instead, it could be the biggest lie of all.

If it turns out deepfake videos *don't* start becoming a more popular source of fake news, that would be great, but—judging by where we are today and how quickly the technology is advancing—I just don't see that happening. I'm betting these deceptive clips will be an increasing headache for anyone who values journalism.

Influence Over Politics

For years, it has been said by commentators and political scientists alike that misinformation is a powerful force in elections in the United States. Following the 2016 election, in which Donald Trump overcame Hillary Clinton to win the presidency, the idea of campaign-based "fake news" received even more attention. Specifically, people began suggesting that President Trump won the 2016 election due to false reports.

For example, Hannah Jane Parkinson, a writer for the *Guardian*, argued on Novemver 14, 2016, that the "alt-right" had "ensnared the electorate using false stories on social media." She contradicted Facebook founder Mark Zuckerberg, who said it was "crazy" to suggest fake news influenced the election, claiming that the fake news "helped Donald Trump win a real election" (Parkinson, 2016). Parkinson wrote:

Many board discussions in the lead up to 8 November advocated this as a strategy. In fact, alt-rightists worried sometimes that Trump's rhetoric was too strong, and might jeopardise his chances. They had a gameplan. The alt-right had an end game; it wasn't for the lulz, and, unlike the left's efforts, it extended to snaring the general electorate.

It's worth noting that, even if alt-righters sought to plant fake news in order to elect Trump, his election wouldn't necessarily prove that they were successful. It's possible that the same set of circumstances could have occurred regardless of the dubious plot. In order to actually find out if fake news could have trumped the voice of the American people, we'd have to have a lot more details about the percentage of fake news stories shared, how they impacted individuals, and more.

In 2017, a study by researchers at Stanford University and New York University clarified what they said was the extent of fake news influence in the 2016 election. Although the authors specifically said they made no determination as to whether misinformation swung the election, they did say that—on average—people didn't read *that* many fake news articles during the Trump-Clinton campaign season. They also noted that their estimates "could underestimate true exposure" because they only measured the number of fake news stories that were read *and* remembered (Allcott & Gentzkow, 2017).

Despite the many clarifications as to the limitations of the study, which only looked at stories that had been debunked by Snopes or Politifact and only if they were shared on Facebook, excluding other social media sites, some seized on those findings and misinterpreted their stated conclusion. One writer for Quartz actually said the study "killed the notion" that fake news caused Trump to win, essentially creating its own inceptioned fake news (Kopf, 2017).

As you might expect, though, there are studies on both sides of this issue. A 2018 study from Ohio State University, for instance, concluded that "fake news may have contributed to Trump's 2016 victory." Those researchers looked at people who voted for Barack Obama in 2012 but who didn't vote for Hillary Clinton in 2016, finding that a significant portion of them (at least 4 percent) had been influenced by anti-Clinton fake news (Gunther, Beck, & Nisbet, 2018).

The point is we may never know whether or not false reports significantly influenced the 2016 election in favor of Trump, but that doesn't mean we haven't learned anything from all these studies. We have learned, for example, that it's all about the *reach* of fake news. Some researchers found the effect was minimal, while others found it was substantial, but they all found that there *was* an effect that could be measured. In other words, we know for a fact that some people *are* influenced by fake news, so much so that they might even change their planned vote. If you live in something that is supposed to (at least superficially) resemble a democracy, that fact should be incredibly scary to you.

If fake news *does* influence the vote, and it's just a matter of degree, then it's also just a matter of time until there's an election in which the results *are close enough* in key districts to have been altered by misinformation. This means that we should do what we can to curb the problem now, before it becomes a national crisis.

Alternatively, if gone unchecked, the fake news industry could proliferate even further, greatly expanding its reach so much that these types of election interferences become commonplace even when the electoral map would otherwise be different. It appears this is already happening, with the number of false stories growing year over year.

Other Negative Effects

In addition to the obvious effects of fraudulent information being spread to every region in the world, there are some ripples being felt more indirectly. For instance, fake news can fan the flames of social conflicts, according to a paper from the University of California, Santa Barbara's CITS program on cultural transitions (Center for Information Technology & Society, n.d.):

> Stories that are untrue and that intentionally mislead readers have caused growing mistrust among American people. In some cases this mistrust results in incivility, protest over imaginary events, or violence. This unravels the fabric of American life, turning neighbor against neighbor.

Some of the consequences of fake news are difficult to track. If someone votes for one candidate over another, how can you really be sure if that was an informed choice or a decision based on false pretenses caused by a misleading pop-up ad they happened to see that morning. We may never know these answers, but it's still good to ask the questions.

These were examples of problems with *fake news*, but what about the issues with *news*?

10 Problems with Journalism

*"I became a journalist because I did not want to rely
on newspapers for information."*

—Christopher Hitchens, English-American writer

I believe journalism, especially quality journalism with proper
ethical safeguards, has the capacity to change the world. It has
been proven to be a force for good, as we discussed earlier on,
and there's no reason to believe that era has come to an end.
Honest journalism, especially investigative journalism looking
into major political policies and actions, is a key to informing
our citizens and holding powerful people responsible for their
misdeeds.

I also believe, however, that there are some major downsides
associated with journalism. Some of these negative aspects of
news writing, which are built into the institution itself, meaning they are a feature and not a "bug" in the software of our
society, could arguably be considered the main contributors to
why mainstream media has seemingly failed so many people

in recent years. Although there *are* other factors, we can't just blame an ignorant readership or political attacks and let that be the end of it.

When considering journalistic follies, especially in the context of a presidential election, it's important not to think in terms of hindsight and what reporters could do better, according to Bharat Anand, author of *The Content Trap* and professor at Harvard Business School (Anand, 2017):

> Thinking that way is tempting, but it misses the mark. The media did exactly what it was designed to do, given the incentives that govern it. It's not that the media sets out to be sensationalist; its business model leads it in that direction. Charges of bias don't make the bias real; it often lies in the eye of the beholder. Fake news and cyberattacks are triggers, not causes. The issues that confront us are structural.

One of these structural issues, I think, is the general inability for competing news organizations to work together.

Disjointed Efforts

One problem with journalism in general is the lack of cooperation that is often exhibited between news agencies. The notoriously independent newsroom inhibits potential stories that could benefit from reporters working together, according to Jonathan Rauch, a Brookings Institution senior fellow:

> In the United States, mainstream media (MSM, as it is sometimes called) have always been allergic to cooperation. The morning paper where I started my career had a fiercely competitive, almost hostile relationship with the local afternoon paper, even though both papers were owned by the same

company and shared a building. Outlets' obsession with independence often works against conducting in-depth investigations and holding public officials to account. An example is how easy it is for a public official to evade hard questions at a press conference by calling on the next journalist, who will almost always change the subject instead of continuing a line of inquiry.

Rauch goes on to say that, even if journalists *wanted* to coordinate with one another, they would have "no ready mechanism to do so."

"Several organizations might sign a joint letter objecting to a government ruling or demanding a document, or they might commission an opinion poll together, but that is about as far as coordination ordinarily goes," he added.

This independence also has its upsides, of course, especially considering the nature of competition and how it tends to motivate. Still, though, a cooperative effort is sometimes needed—and right now it's not really possible.

Unfortunately, this isn't the only problem with the journalism landscape.

Easily Distracted

In addition to being notoriously bad at cooperation, the press—in general—has difficulty focusing on in-depth topics for long periods of time. This isn't necessarily the fault of reporters, specifically; it's the nature of humanity to be interested in the next thing. Journalists simply cater to the general public—I'd argue a little too much, at times.

Still, this tendency of the media to be easily distracted—even by more frivolous matters—hasn't gone unnoticed by people in political power who want to change the public narrative to something that is better for them. Some have even been pretty open about doing just that. Take Hillary Clinton, for example, who once said, "If I want to knock a story off the front page, I just change my hairstyle." So, it's clear this is a loophole that leaders are able to take advantage of.

The biggest issue with media distraction, in my opinion, is that it's so easily abused by powerful individuals and groups who hope to manipulate the public—and often in ways that are less innocent than the Hillary Clinton quote suggests. In fact, allegations of media distraction are incredibly rampant in U.S. politics. Jon Stewart, former host of *The Daily Show*, said President Trump intentionally uses the media's tendency to be distracted against itself. Specifically, Stewart told CNN's Christiane Amanpour that Trump would "bait" the press by attacking it, which would lure reporters into a fight that isn't about the policies of the government.

In part, Stewart said, this happens because President Trump appeals to reporters' egos. He explained:

He baits them, and they dive in. They take it personally, and now he's changed the conversation to, not that his policies are silly or not working . . . it's all about the fight.

By accusing the media of being "fake news," Stewart says, he's able to change the "conversation" to something that can score him political points as opposed to something that could politically damage him. And this isn't even unique; similar allegations have arisen about several other political figures spanning across all ideologies and parties.

Some media distraction is more passive in nature. If we go back to March 2016, for instance, we can see an article from *Time* saying Donald Trump "distracted the media from John Kasich," a moderate Republican he faced off against in the

2016 election (Klein, 2016). In that case, though, the claim wasn't that Trump himself called a reporter claiming to be somebody else—something else Trump has been previously accused of (Farrington, 2016). Instead, *Time* writer Joe Klein said the media was "caught up in Trumpery" through no fault of the man himself.

This is also an aspect of journalism that has been recognized and criticized by many charities, who have reportedly said that journalists are necessary for coverage of important events but are also easily distracted. For example, European reports reveal the difficulty some charities say they have had in getting journalists to cover certain major issues that may have required more nuance (Clarke, Leach, & van der Zee, 2015). Some reporters, spokespeople have said, tend to quickly move on once an issue has lost its initial spark, even if there is more to uncover.

I also think this distraction works both ways, in that the general public is frequently prone to distraction even when journalists are properly thorough. In this sense, it's not so much a problem with journalism as a problem with humanity itself. Still, under proper conditions, the journalism industry could devise a system to better fight against this tendency.

Outdated Model

Another problem with journalism that has consistently contributed to its ongoing issues is the traditional media's outdated model and unquestioningly slow adaption to change. Anecdotally, I think about a niche newspaper where I worked right out of college beginning in 2011. It was a print paper, complete with a 5:00 p.m. daily deadline, and it didn't publish anything throughout the day. Its online presence was abysmal, with some content being uploaded on its website the next day but nothing ever going up before its printed counterpart. As a recent college graduate just starting out, I was surprised to see that the traditional paper still had a printing press—let alone that it was its primary method of delivery. Although this was a respected newspaper, its circulation began to dwindle as its sophisticated readership started to move to faster online content services.

Of course, this phenomenon is larger than that particular paper where I used to work. In fact, in July 2012, one year after I began working for this daily paper, the *New York Times* published a piece indicating that the "newspaper industry is running out of time to adapt to" the internet and other digital technologies (Carr, 2012). In it, the author—the late *Times* columnist David Carr—compared the newspaper industry to the automobile and steel industries, pointing to "underfunded pension plans, unserviceable debt and legacy manufacturing processes and union agreements." He also said that pay cuts and the rising errors that follow (journalists "constantly being asked to do more with less") were contributing to the decline of newspapers.

This slow adaptation causes reduced readership, which leads to more cuts and more errors, which again leads to more losses. It's a vicious circle. And if that wasn't bad enough, the journalism industry is funded by advertisers, which tend to head for the hills when there are signs of distress. So, as we discussed previously, those advertisers have options. And one of those options is to look at what *is* getting clicks and readership, and invest wherever that is. After all, that will get the best results for traffic and success in ads. You probably see where I'm going with this: a lot of advertisers are abandoning the mainstream outlets for sites producing misinformation.

Dominic Carter, chief commercial officer at News UK, has weighed in on the debate. He said "credible news brands" are getting edged out by fast news producers that don't necessarily care enough to check accuracy. This, in turn, can open people up to false information (Chahal, 2017). Carter told *Marketing Week*:

> We don't have a fake news problem, we have an issue with getting advertisers to understand the value of credible trusted news versus an audience, which is playing to the hands of the distributors.

A writer at the *New Yorker* has also said that journalists who "survived the print purge" are *still* being forced to adapt or die in the wake of the continued growth of the fake news industry (made worse by the archaic ad-based system). She asked the important question, "Does journalism have a future?"

It's my opinion that journalism *does* have a future, and that we can all be a part of that, but it may take some amendments to the structure of the current system.

That being said, there are some aspects of journalism that are controversial for good reason and can't necessarily be changed.

Controversial Interviews

There are a number of different landmines you can trigger in journalism, but nowhere is there more of a risk of explosion than in talking to people who may be considered unethical.

One aspect of the job that puts many journalists in stressful situations is the nature of the all-important controversial interview. Interviews themselves are critical to good reporting because they help reveal information straight from the horse's mouth, as it were. But there is a line you must walk when you're interviewing certain high-profile individuals, because there will always be the criticism that you are providing the figure with a platform, even if you adamantly disagree with them on every issue. I myself have encountered this when interviewing a famous white supremacist in an attempt to dismantle his ideas, expose him, and show the flaws in his reasoning to the public. When I saw that he was promoting the interview in a positive manner, I deleted it and never looked back.

That's not to say that the controversial interview can't be done with success. Consider the now-famous Gayle King interview with R. Kelly, who had been accused of various forms of sexual assault and even sexual slavery for years before that. King was initially criticized for providing a platform to the alleged abuser, and not to the people who were allegedly victims, but the interview ultimately allowed the public to see an "unhinged" side of Kelly, who had consistently denied culpability. Shortly after the interview, Kelly was arrested, and King said she was "not surprised" by it (Jensen, 2019).

Visibility arguments aside, interviewing subjects who are enemies of the general public is incredibly important. There's always the possibility, for instance, that they can provide ammunition for law enforcement officers seeking warrants or indictments.

Aside from that, certain controversial interviews can contribute to the cultural understanding of a particular situation. If you head to the Jewish Virtual Library, for instance, you'll find an interesting piece about a holocaust survivor, Tolvi Blatt, who interviewed a death camp supervisor named Karl Frenzel. This was the only time such an interview occurred, and Blatt was forced to limit his emotions to prepare, according to historian Eric Gartman (Gartman, n.d.):

> To tolerate meeting with the murderer, Blatt tried to distance himself emotionally, to act only as an objective writer carrying out important historical research.

Frenzel wanted to ask forgiveness from Blatt, after claiming he regretted his actions while at the same time downplaying them, Gartman added. Still, Blatt was able to successfully get the information he needed and publish his historical account one year after the death of Frenzel.

More on interviewing controversial subjects can be learned from Louis Theroux, a documentary filmmaker who specializes in these kinds of taboo interactions. He told the *Columbia Journalism Review* that he gets to know people who have questionable, controversial, and even hateful views, and helps others understand their motivations better. He also said his non-confrontational style has helped people open up about key facts he needed to find out for a successful interview, including white supremacists who felt "totally emotionally open" (The Editors, JR, 2017):

> From thinking I was going into a hostile environment, I was aware that I was suddenly in this environment in which they felt totally emotionally open and that I could have a conversation that was wholly other and, in an odd way, human with them.

I've made mistakes regarding interviewing controversial subjects, but I've also had some victories, including with a messed-up cult.

If you've ever seen a group of religious people on a sidewalk with picket signs that say, "God hates f*gs," you're probably familiar with the Westboro Baptist Church. Based in Topeka, Kansas, the church is mostly made up of a few families who live together in a massive cult-like compound. For an earlier book, called *No Sacred Cows: Investigating Myths, Cults, and the Supernatural,* I interviewed three current and former members of the Westboro Baptist Church, an infamous hate group. Not only did I reveal information that had never been reported about the group's teachings, specifically with regard to how they learn about other religions, but I also challenged them on several key components of their flawed doctrine. The emphasis on the interviews with the former members, who had stopped spreading hate, helped make sure that they were widely accepted and even appreciated.

Despite all the problems and potential for mistakes within journalism, and the influx of fake news, it's important to note that it's worth saving. And it won't be that hard for us, either. We just have to get better at understanding what good reporting looks like, and stop empowering imposters.

11 Identifying Fake News

"Having fact checkers is great, because we should have a sense of what is true and not true in the world. But just the existence of fact checkers alone is not going to ensure that the truth wins out."

—Adam Berinsky, political scientist

If fake news imitates *real* news, and is meant to evoke the exact same feelings, it becomes increasingly important to learn to distinguish between them. In fact, as we've discussed in earlier chapters, it's entirely possible that telling the difference is a life-or-death situation. But it can also be one of the most difficult things we do in our daily lives.

One way in which purveyors of misinformation disguise their false and biased claims as legitimate, researched news is to throw up the "article" on a web template that resembles that of a local news site. To the untrained eye, these often boiler-plate websites can look essentially the same as the real thing, and local news is one of the most trusted mediums in the world.

In fact, some companies have taken this method to the

next level. Fake news provider Locality Labs, for instance, has published a print newspaper in a town in Illinois with the local school district's logo in order to gain the favor of the local community. The paper—one of many efforts by Locality Labs on the fake news front around the world—went to great lengths to disguise its true source of funding, a right-wing thinktank, and pretend to be associated with the school. Called the *Hinsdale School News*, the paper even names Hinsdale Township High School District 86 and Community Consolidated School District 181 on page one (Lannom, 2019).

Instead of district-approved content, however, the paper reportedly provided an extremely agenda-driven accounting of certain high-profile policies and issues. Specifically, the paper campaigned *against* a push for a $140 million bond for school improvements.

The plan worked incredibly well, in part because of the paper's resemblance to *trusted* media in the local community. They had most of the trappings that brought out a feeling of respect and ethics. But the fact that they were able to produce something that *looked like* the real thing doesn't mean there weren't *some* red flags that should have been noticed by informed and motivated truth seekers. For instance, a sizable majority of the stories *opposed* funding for the school it pretended to support. If that wasn't a big enough clue, the stories published in the faux newspaper mostly lacked a *byline*.

Byline Behavior

For a journalist, a byline is everything. It's how a reporter gets credit and how they announce authorship to the world. Aside from that, and more importantly in this context, a byline provides you with transparency in several ways. Any legitimate reporter, for instance, understands the importance of disclosing potential conflicts of interest. If you don't have a byline listed and readers can't see the name of a particular writer, how can they see if the author of a political piece, for instance, has donated millions to the opposing candidate's campaign? Similarly, how could readers see if a reporter is employed by a company that has a stake in the outcome of the situation they're covering? These are key facts that make a byline so important in legitimate journalism. So, if you are reading an article and it doesn't say anything about who wrote it, it should give you pause. That fact alone doesn't necessarily mean the article is fake, but it *does* mean you should ask some questions.

It's not just a lack of a byline you want to look for. After all, a lot of fake news publishers know that it looks shady to have no byline, so they include a fake name that won't draw attention. But for a curious reader, that seemingly random name could just mean there is investigating to be done. At the bare minimum, you *should* be able to click their name and see previous articles they've written. If you take some time to peruse through those, it could give you some hints as to whether or not the reporter is writing from an agenda and distorting facts.

It's important to note that a lack of a byline, or even the use of a pseudonym, doesn't *always* mean you're reading fake news. There are many legitimate circumstances under which a reporter or contributor would want to remain anonymous, so this must only be treated as part of the question. For example, if you are writing a report about your boss and don't want them to retaliate against you, you may choose to hide your identity. If you are a reporter who is doing this, it helps to be as transparent as possible by including a disclaimer explaining that there are good reasons for your decision to remain anonymous.

You may also want to look out for other designators that are common with the real media. For example, does the author have an email or Twitter profile listed anywhere? Is the author identified by a job title, such as "reporter" or "correspondent," or are they listed as a subject matter expert? Is there an editor listed for the story? These are all important questions to ask and, taken together, they could help you determine if what you're reading is the real deal.

Check the Site

In addition to checking in on the author, you'll want to analyze the website on which the article appears. First, check the URL in the address bar. Is it the one you thought it was, or is it trying to pass itself off as a more legitimate news agency? One famous fake news site, abcnews.com.co, replicates abcnews.go.com as closely as possible in order to get unearned social media shares.

A lot of fake news sites will use Wordpress and other free or inexpensive personal blog-hosting platforms, but that certainly doesn't mean everything published there is misinformation. In fact, news is being broken in blog format more and more regularly as the age of information gives more people a voice. The host site should only be considered as a small part of the larger inquiry into veracity.

More important than the platform is taking into account the specific policies and procedures of the site you're reviewing. For instance, if you scroll to the bottom of the article, does the site list intellectual property info, privacy warnings, and contact details? These and other bottom-of-site options have become mainstays of traditional media sites that have at least some form of editorial process, making them a good place to start out.

Another important aspect about the site is whether it provides the option to learn more about the editorial process. Does the site describe what its editors do, how to request corrections, and where it gets funding? These are all the hallmarks of the sites you know best and trust most, and fake news publishers aren't often committed enough to mimic the details when it comes down to the fine print items.

Check the Content

Once you verify that the site is reliable, the next step is to independently check that the content itself isn't "fake news." For starters, you'll probably want to check the coverage depth across other credible news sites. If it's an important piece of news, there's a good chance that someone else will be covering it. So, using key words, use your search engine of choice to look for the news subject and see if other people are talking about it. Of course, on certain exclusive stories, it's possible you will only find one source when it's legitimate, but those cases are few and far between.

In addition to checking for coverage of the general issue, you'll probably want to investigate specific claims you read that seem dubious. If an article has links and sources, follow them and check them. If it doesn't, that's a red flag all by itself. In that case, you'll want to search independently for the claims made, and see if you can find supporting or disproving evidence independent of the article.

In addition to written content, you can also check the photos and videos placed within the article. For images, it's as easy as dragging and dropping the item into Google to do a reverse image search, which will check for duplicates published elsewhere online. While not completely dispositive, this will give you an idea of what you're working with.

Equal Opportunity Misinformation

You might think identifying fake news is something you're great at, and that you don't need help with it, but I think we all could use a boost. It's important to understand that fake news isn't a problem of one particular class or generation. It has existed for as long as real news has, and its victims consist of everyone—including thought leaders and the political elite. Lawmakers fall for fake news all the time, but some instances are more memorable than others. For example, we saw Congressman Steve King (R-Iowa) come down with a textbook case of fake news fever in November 2019.

King, who earlier that same year compared his struggles to those of Jesus after the lawmaker was stripped of his committee assignments for making racist comments (Feldscher, 2019), was attempting to identify a whistleblower in a high-profile case against President Trump when he fell for a conspiracy theory. Actually, he mistakenly mixed two unproven conspiracy theories together into one when he posted a collage of images featuring the son of billionaire George Soros with prominent Democrats, according to Ali Breland of *Mother Jones* (Breland, 2019):

> While King has levied attacks at George Soros in the past, it's not likely his tweet was an attempt to rope him or his son into the Ukraine scandal—instead it seems that King fell for a right-wing hoax website's misinformation.

King likely got the misinformation from a site that was designed to deceive. They used methods common among peddlers of fake news, including mimicking trusted local news networks, Breland reported:

> The websites which distributed the composite image of Soros were designed to appear like local news outlets—a common tactic among people seeking to spread disinformation and misinformation. The strategy was used by Russian trolls to influence American politics on social media in 2016, and has

been replicated by others, including different countries and private, for-profit hyperpartisan news ad farms.

It becomes increasingly clear that King was the victim of fake news when you consider the fact that he deleted the tweet almost immediately after someone pointed out that the person pictured was actually Soros and not the whistleblower.

Of course, this is just one drop in a sea of fake news blunders from politicians in the United States and around the globe. One of my favorite examples, though, involves a website that doesn't intend to deceive at all: the Onion, which has been providing political satire stories for decades. I'm talking about when Congressman John Fleming (R-LA) mistakenly shared an Onion article indicating Planned Parenthood had opened an $8 million "Abortionplex" to help them "terminate unborn lives with an efficiency never before thought possible," thinking it was real. Fleming posted a caption with the article, writing, "More on Planned Parenthood, abortion by the wholesale" (Grandoni, 2012).

Indeed, fake news permeates every party and branch of government. In one case, Energy Secretary Rick Perry, one of the people responsible for the United States' arsenal of nuclear weapons, fell for a privacy hoax on Instagram. He posted a fraudulent chain message that claimed to exempt the poster from invasions of privacy by the social media platform (Mack, 2019). That Instagram post was a recycled version of an old Facebook "copyright" hoax, yet it still tricked a number of celebrities, including P!nk, T.I., Julia Roberts, Debra Messing, Usher, Julianne Moore, and more, but none of them wielded the power that Perry did.

Dan Solomon of *Texas Monthly* pointed out that Perry isn't the only Texas official to "squander credibility by sharing an internet hoax" (Solomon, 2019):

Governor Greg Abbott has a history of swallowing hoaxes—from fake Churchill quotes to fake Jerry Jones quotes to, more seriously, Jade Helm. The staff of agriculture commissioner Sid Miller, whose social media presence is a mess of memes and hoaxes, told reporters last year, "We post hundreds of things a week" and "We put stuff out there" by way of explanation. Of course, both Abbott and Miller won re-election last fall by 13 and 5 percentage points, respectively, so the cost of burnt credibility might ultimately be minimal.

In case you thought spreading fake news was isolated to one political party, let's take a look at the other side of the aisle. One Democrat and former presidential candidate, Marianne Williamson, became known for spreading dangerous misinformation and fringe pseudoscience. While Williamson, a self-help author, has claimed to be "proscience" (Sherfinski, 2019), she has also been criticized for positions on antidepressants and vaccination that some say "can literally kill people." More broadly, Williamson has claimed in her book that "sickness is an illusion and does not exist" (Beauchamp, 2019). This is a textbook pseudoscientific claim.

Political figures sharing dangerous fake news may not cause damage to their chances during an election season, but it *does* cause harm to society. In fact, a Pew Research Center survey gave some insight into just how big of a problem misinformation really is when it found that more Americans labeled false stories as a very big problem for the country than thought the same about terrorism, illegal immigration, racism, and more (Mitchell, Gottfried, Stocking, Walker, & Fedeli, 2019).

So, if Americans are starting to see how big of a problem fake news really is, how can we minimize the chances that we fall in a trap just like the people above? Here are some things to take into consideration.

Red flags

- **Video isolation.** This is a technique used by fake news purveyors to separate the context of an event from a clip. By using a real video, but snipping away any explanations as to what happened, an individual or group can make a believable snippet of fake news that actually convinces people.

- **Typos and errors.** While it's true that everyone makes mistakes, and you can find typographical errors in any mainstream publication, a pattern of errors in spelling or punctuation on an otherwise legitimate-appearing website could mean that you're reading a website meant to trick its readers into believing it is a quality news article.

- **Storytelling style.** Journalists use a distinct style—detached, fact-based, and very often based on an inverted pyramid method invented more than a hundred years ago—when writing their news reports. If you're reading something that looks like a news story, and you start to notice overly emotional language, that could be a red flag that you're reading a false report, or at least one tainted by a strong bias that could affect quality.

- **Sources.** Does the article you're reading make a lot of claims, but not source the information as is typically done? That could be a hint that you're not reading the work of a real journalist. If the piece *does* list sources, then check them out. Does the source they list *actually* say what they claim? Source misrepresentations are key to the entire fake news industry.

- **Excessive ads.** A lot of mainstream news agencies are funded by advertising, so the existence of ads doesn't necessarily mean you're looking at fake news. That being said, excessive ads—ads that block content or maybe even give you viruses—are a huge red flag. This usually means they don't care about people reading the content, and instead are just focusing on getting more clicks. That system inherently leads to bad journalism.

- **Is the news too good to be true?** If you're reading an article, and thinking to yourself, "Wow, this is great news. Huge! I have to share it," it could be an indicator that it was *designed* to give you that exact impression. Fake news purveyors know that positive news, especially wins for particular political sides, get the most clicks and shares. So, they might make up or exaggerate things in order to get monetary boosts.

These are just some of the red flags to look out for when you're consuming news, but helping your friends and family to do the same thing can be slightly more complex.

12 Helping Misguided Loved Ones

"The public doesn't know what to believe anymore. We don't know what stories are supposedly true, this idea of 'fake news.' We watch it on what I guess you would call a split-focus. It's half entertainment and half mystery."

—Barry Levinson, filmmaker

When it comes to fake news, we've all been a victim at one time or another, even if we don't know it. But there's a difference between sharing a couple of articles per month because you were too busy to fact-check, and someone who basically lives in an alternate reality because they pretty much *only* consume faulty information. You might think that I'm exaggerating, but the fact is that false information may actually be able to cause delusions, according to one study (Murphy, Loftus, Hofstein Grady, Levine, & Greene, 2019). Specifically, the researchers found that people may form *false memories* after seeing fake news, especially if the misinformation lines up with a subject's prior beliefs:

Almost half of the sample reported a false memory for at least one fabricated event, with more than one third of participants reporting a specific memory of the event. A subsequent warning about possible misinformation slightly reduced rates of false memories but did not eliminate these effects.

This study gives us *some* insight into what we can do to prevent false news leading to false memories, but there's still more to it than that. We have to find out what's so appealing about fake news for those who share it, as well as learn more about why it's so difficult for people to admit when they're wrong. Finding these answers is part of the journey toward combatting misinformation, and helping loved ones escape its clutches.

If someone you care about fits this profile, it can put you in an incredibly uncomfortable position. We have an instinctive need to help our loved ones, but they could also be suffering from cognitive dissonance, which would make it difficult for them to accept your assistance. The deeper they get into the swamp of fake news, the more difficult it can be for those who love them to pull them out.

Helping anyone see they are wrong is a difficult task, especially in an era of heightened partisan politics. When it comes to someone addicted to misinformation, there's no guaranteed way to snap them out of it. That being said, there are certainly some things we can do to help, even if we don't see results immediately. And it begins with *attitude*.

Making Them Care

If you see someone you know consistently sharing reports from sites with a bad track record for accuracy and a history of spreading dangerous rumors, it may be tempting to confront them. And most often, this looks something like this: "WRONG. This post is bullshit and you should know better than to share it."

We've all been guilty of posting something like this in response to an aggravating piece of fake news, but that doesn't mean it's the right way to handle the situation. In fact, it might pay off in the long run not to *correct* them right away at all.

Let me be clear: I'm *not* saying you should let it slide when loved ones perpetuate harmful and false narratives. I'm saying the best way to *stop* that behavior is by addressing the underlying issues. The first of those being that they should *care about the difference* between true and false stories, and want to improve the overall accuracy of their posts and daily speech.

You might think that's obvious, and that pretty much everyone wants to avoid spreading misinformation, but that's just not true. Or it's not entirely true, anyway.

The fact is that most people who spread fake news probably don't do so in order to intentionally mislead anyone. More often than not, they are driven by *emotional* motives, and the veracity of the subject doesn't factor in very much. If there's an article that targets a politician or celebrity they don't like, they'll be more likely to share it without fact-checking, in part because the negative material seems believable and in part because of a knee-jerk reaction to attack their perceived opponent.

An article from Vice uses a specific fake news story, a report alleging President Donald Trump didn't have an earpiece in to listen to language translations at an important meeting of world leaders, to drive the point home. The piece states that, when confronted with the fact that the article was fake, someone who posted it didn't really seem to care (Friedlander, 2019):

> Yannick LeJacq, a California-based writer, admitted to me that he was one of the thousands of people who shared the story on social media, taking to Facebook to post a link from a website he hadn't heard of before. The implication, he said,

was that Trump "wasn't even bothering to listen to the translations coming through from the other world leaders."

. . . .

LeJacq told me he discovered the article was false soon after
he posted it, then tried to warn a Facebook friend who had
also shared a similar article that it was 'essentially a fake news
item.' They didn't seem to care. "They got huffy and said
something to the effect of, 'Well, he definitely hasn't listened
to people tons of times anyways, so what's the harm?'"

There's certainly an element of cognitive dissonance here,
hence the defensive reply, but it's not as though the individual
denied that the post was fake and clung to the falsehood. Instead, they accepted the reality but insisted spreading the fake
news did no harm considering they believe the subject of the
piece is guilty of the reported conduct at least in spirit. This
is called self-justification, and it's a lot easier in this particular
context if you don't fully respect the importance of telling the
truth more generally.

Getting someone to *care* about the truth is not an easy task,
but it can be done if you have time and patience. It will most
often be part of an ongoing dialogue, and not a simple one-off
conversation.

There are a variety of ways to get there, and each solution
should be considered on a case-by-case basis, but one method
I've had success with has been *personalization*. Basically, I get the
person to admit and understand that the truth is important to
them *on a personal level*. If they don't want people to lie to them,
even if those lies reinforce their beliefs about something, then
why would they want to be the one contributing to the problem
in the other direction?

Another way to educate your friends or family on this issue is to make them understand the severity of the fake news

problem itself, and how they are contributing to it and making it even worse. If they see how misinformation can risk reputations and lives, as discussed previously, they may want to be more wary about the unchecked ideas they put out there.

Help Them Avoid Echo Chambers

One problem with unreliable sources of information is the isolation they often cause from other, legitimate news. Whether that is a direct result of a smear campaign from the fake news site, or an inadvertent effect caused by cognitive dissonance when watching the news, it's common for those who are addicted to fake news to stick to a few sources with highly similar content.

This is called an echo chamber, and even if you are *right* about something, it can keep you from growing. If you're wrong, however, things are even worse. That's when the same little bubble of similar thoughts can breed, and lead to a cycle of lazily recycled ignorance.

To prevent this from happening in my life, I intake news from a variety of different sites, including those with ideologically opposing points of view. I make a conscious effort to see what each side of the political spectrum is talking about at any given time, and then compare notes. Now, does this mean that I believe everything all of these news sources say about every subject? Not even close. In fact, I tend to take *all* news with a grain of salt until I've had time to independently research it for myself. But having a larger palette of options allows me to be more informed about what everyone is thinking.

Journalist and *ABC World News Tonight* anchor David Muir has spoken out about the harms of echo chambers, and pointed out how social media tends to contribute to the problem (Herbert, 2017).

On *Jimmy Kimmel Live*, Muir said:

Your Facebook feed, which is essentially curated, your news feed it's called, but those are your interests, your likes, so you often get the viewpoints you're expecting to get fed back to you. I think there is a danger when it comes to fake news because there is some fake news out there, but there's also a danger when you only hear back to you the beliefs you already have.

This is a good place to start for helping your loved ones because it's relatively simple. You don't have to convince anyone that they are wrong about something that they care about, or convince them to distrust the media they already like. All you have to do is gradually introduce them to new sources of information, growing their sphere of awareness and making them less likely to get trapped in the deadly Chamber of Echoes.

You could even make a thinking exercise out of it by encouraging them to distrust everything they *want* to be true to help account for confirmation bias. In other words, because our brains are trained to seek out information that agrees with our own ideas, it may be helpful to account for that by playing devil's advocate against our subconscious. If you see something you strongly agree with, assume it's false and then listen—I mean *really* listen—to the arguments of those who say it's false. If they start making sense, it may be good to reevaluate some things.

Travel and Reading

If you are dealing with someone who has the means to travel, yet does not to any meaningful degree, curing a fake news addiction could be as easy as booking a flight. Okay, so that's a bit of an exaggeration, but there is a grain of truth to that. The reason echo chambers are bad is because we don't get exposure to other ideas, right? And what is the best way to hear ideas that don't comport with those you hear every day? Traveling internationally. Mark Twain agreed. He wrote in *Innocents Abroad*:

> Travel is fatal to prejudice, bigotry, and narrow-mindedness, and many of our people need it sorely on these accounts. Broad, wholesome, charitable views of men and things cannot be acquired by vegetating in one little corner of the earth all one's lifetime.

Twain's quote certainly catches the ear in a positive way, but is the advice actually supported by science? According to one team of researchers, the answer is, "Yes."

A 2013 study published in *Social Psychological and Personality Science* (Cao, Galinsky, & Maddux, 2013) found that the number of countries someone visits can increase generalized trust. In other words, according to one of the authors of the study, one's breadth of travel can make them more trusting of others. That includes visiting countries that are dissimilar to our own (Dolan, 2013). If fear is a big reason many people cling to fake news, as we discussed previously, then this potential attitude shift could make a difference.

For those who can't afford to hop on a plane and visit a different country, I recommend the next best thing: reading. I don't mean reading conspiracy theory websites, or even a newspaper. I'm talking about someone reading novels and nonfiction works from various perspectives, and throwing themselves into entirely new worlds. If done right, this can give you some of the exact same types of experiences as traveling abroad, but without maxing out your credit cards.

Helping Them Think

Earlier in the book, we covered self-regulatory, governmental, and technological solutions to the misinformation situation in which we find ourselves. Guy P. Harrison, author of *Think Before You Like*, disagrees with those tactics for improvement. Instead, he favors an approach that more directly addresses the issues of gullibility and naiveté (Harrison, 2019):

> I disagree with calls for governments and corporations to clean up the mess that is online fake news. First, there is a conflict of interest—these are often the sources of dishonest content. Second, freedom of speech is an invaluable concept that should not be weakened. Third, it is a defeatist victim mentality to expect someone else to protect your brain. Police your own thoughts. Don't be such an easy mark. Good thinking is not as difficult as you may imagine.[15]

Harrison recommends several defenses for preventing consumption of fake news, including "be skeptical of everything" and "consider the source." He also suggests that readers should "slow down," writing:

> When reading news, it's wise to withhold fully accepting a claim or digging in on a position until you know more, preferably from multiple sources. Did you just read that Kanye West kicked a puppy? Wait and gather more intel before deleting all of his songs from your playlist.
>
> Never forget that an important component of news is speed, never more so than today. But while speed is a priority for news media companies, it doesn't have to be yours.

---

15. Jestin Coler, who runs a number of fake news sites based on ads, including NationalReport.net and USAToday.com.co, said something similar: "Some of this has to fall on the readers themselves. The consumers of content have to be better at identifying this stuff. We have a whole nation of media-illiterate people. Really, there needs to be something done." So, while it may not necessarily be all of our mindset, we know at least some fake news sellers do think this way.

Harrison also encourages readers to find out if other news outlets are covering a particular story, learn the difference between opinion and news, research the URL of the source in question, and read all articles before sharing them.

Media Literacy

Younger generations often take for granted that they understand technology and new media, meaning older people can be left behind in defending themselves from the onslaught of misinformation. In fact, a study in *Science Advances* found that, while most Facebook users didn't share any fake news articles in 2016, people over the age of sixty-five were almost seven times more likely to share misinformation online than the youngest group in the experiment (Guess, Nagler, & Tucker, 2019). In the "data and method" section, the researchers wrote:

> This is true even when holding other characteristics—including education, ideology, and partisanship—constant. No other demographic characteristic seems to have a consistent effect on sharing fake news, making our age finding that much more notable.

This phenomenon is mostly expected for older individuals. If you've ever helped your grandma set up a printer or tried to teach your parents how to update their phones, you know that technological innovations are generally more difficult for older generations, and with fake news coming in increasingly nuanced forms, it just adds to the problem. That being said, that doesn't mean there aren't exceptions, nor does it mean there aren't options to help keep senior citizens safe and well informed on the internet, a place where viruses and fake news are everywhere.

One group that has done work to counteract this effect is the League of Women Voters, which has hosted a series of "What's True? Media Literacy & Fake News" events in California, including in Palo Alto and in Santa Maria (Best, 2018). At the Palo Alto event, the league reportedly brought in voices from the tech community, academia, and more. The speakers came from Google, Facebook, Data for Democracy, the Institute for the Future, the Center for Information Technology Research in the Interest of Society (UC Berkeley), and Stanford University, according to the league's blog (Little-Saña, 2018).

Advice from those experts included everything from the obvious, such as "think before you share," to keeping a list of easy tips at hand as an "earthquake preparedness kit" for so-called fake news. Google's Dan Russell further suggested that people should "make that one extra search" to double-check a reported piece of information before simply believing it.

Sarah McGrew of Stanford University also explained that it's not *just* seniors who need media literacy training. In fact, she said, students are especially susceptible to false information. Our youngest generation may be tech savvy, but they aren't necessarily information savvy, she explained. In order to evaluate political news, McGrew said we should be asking three simple questions:

1. Who is behind the information?

2. What is the evidence for the position?

3. What do other sources say?

While younger people may be getting fooled by fake news, studies still show the problem is more serious among older generations, who also vote more than their younger, misinformed counterparts.

Renée DiResta, a 2019 Mozilla Fellow in Media, Misinformation, and Trust who has worked on this issue with the League of Women Voters and spoke at the event in Palo Alto, told me in an interview:

> Individuals who did not come of age in the digital environment and did not receive much training in understanding who wrote an article, what a reputable site is, etc., are more frequently misled or duped. This is similarly replicated in studies of online scams.

To help (possibly older) relatives and friends who might be falling for misinformation online, DiResta suggests that a simple discussion in private could do the trick. In an email, she wrote:

> I think gentle private corrections work better than public callouts—sending a DM or note to say that something is false, a source is disreputable, etc. I think educating them that people are not always what they appear to be in messages or on Twitter, and sending them articles with social media best-practices, can ensure they have a positive experience and don't fall prey to scams or bad actors.

DiResta said there are different types of online misinformation, and that she has different advice depending on what the individual is actually experiencing:

- **Scams.** There are many different online scams, many of which involve obtaining your personal information. To be prepared for those, DiResta recommends looking out for "any stranger trying to start a relationship, sending unsolicited chat messages, asking for money, directing you to a site that does not have your best interest at heart."

- **Misinformation.** This is probably the most common piece of "fake news" online, and to help others watch out for it, DiResta says we should be "stressing the importance of fact-checking things that are highly sensationalized with a look at a known reputable entity's website or a factchecker such as Snopes or PolitiFact."

- **Disinformation.** Perhaps the most insidious of all false claims one can encounter online is disinformation, and it is the most difficult to nail down since it's so often coming from what some consider the most trusted source: a government. DiResta says it's more difficult to spot disinformation, but that making loved ones "aware that these campaigns exist" and that they are targeting people with interests they might share is "helpful."

Lastly, DiResta says she associates the internet and senior media literacy with her parents, who she wants to be safe:

> It's been great for keeping in touch with family, but I try to make sure they have high digital literacy and use strong passwords and understand privacy settings. Reviewing privacy settings—or setting them up on older relatives' behalf—is also useful.

Some insights on this issue can also be gleaned from Mike Caulfield, director of blended and networked learning at Washington State University, Vancouver. He teaches media literacy to kids, and reports many of them sincerely want to know how to help the older people in their lives with the same.

Caulfield, who says older people are more likely to inadvertently share extremist iconography they don't fully comprehend, says reaching these individuals may take a more personalized approach than most others. For instance, he says, you should reach out to them privately when you see them post extremist images or misinformed views to help them understand the broader context (Silverman, 2019):

> There's a good chance your family member doesn't understand that and might be horrified at what they're sharing. And so there's a point to intervene and let people know, "Hey, I know, this was probably not what you meant, but . . ."

I talked to Caulfield, who confirmed that older people are more likely to share political disinformation, and possibly health misinformation, as well. He also said technology is a factor when it comes to sharing disinformation, but that the generation divide is more complex than that. In that interview, Caulfield told me:

> I think it's more likely that adults, who are engaged in political life more fully in so many other ways, happen to be exposed to more of this and are more interested in sharing political content in general. Additionally, they are more likely to suffer from social isolation, and a number of other issues that predict engagement with disinformation.

Since the demographic elements aren't going to change, we're "left with remedies around teaching people to be more web literate," Caulfield noted, adding that the same types of internet education can be applied to different generations:

> And yes, I think the same web literacy that helps older people can help younger people as well. I teach faculty and students to do this, and there's surprisingly little difference in the skills they need but don't have.

When asked how to best help older relatives and friends not fall for fake news, Caulfield said it's all "contextual" because there are often larger issues at play, as well:

> If your father is sliding down a white supremacist rabbit hole your approach is going to be different than if he is sharing a death hoax. The biggest thing I'd say is concentrate on the strength of your relationship. Assuming your dad or mom isn't a person of influence, it's probably the case that their small role in disinformation doesn't cause all that much harm. So it doesn't have to be solved right away.

Caulfield added that he recommends the "SIFT" method, which includes the following steps (Caulfield, 2019):

- **Stop.** The simplest of the four steps—called "moves"—is to stop and ask whether you know the website or other source of information. "If you don't have that information, use the other moves to get a sense of what you're looking at. Don't read it or share media until you know what it is."

- **Investigate the source.** In line with the first move, the investigation prong involves looking into what you read before you read it. You should at least have a general idea of what you're reading and from what perspective it is coming, when possible, according to Caulfield. "Now, you don't have to do a Pulitzer prize-winning investigation into a source before you engage with it. But if you're reading a piece on economics by a Nobel prize-winning economist, you should know that before you read it. Conversely, if you're watching a video on the many benefits of milk consumption that was put out by the dairy industry, you want to know that as well."

- **Find trusted coverage.** For this move, you want to

change focuses from the *source* to the *claim*. Instead of researching the context of the article, you look into the claim itself and see if you can find coverage from another, more trusted source. "If you get an article that says koalas have just been declared extinct from the Save the Koalas Foundation, your best bet might not be to investigate the source, but to go out and find the best source you can on this topic, or, just as importantly, to scan multiple sources and see what the expert consensus seems to be."

- **Trace claims, quotes, and media back to the original context.** This move requires you to understand the context of what you're reading. A lot of fake news is successful because it uses true events and merely switches around key details, so by understanding the facts behind the purported news item you can make sure you aren't fooled. "Much of what we find on the internet has been stripped of context. Maybe there's a video of a fight between two people with Person A as the aggressor. But what happened before that? What was clipped out of the video and what stayed in? Maybe there's a picture that seems real but the caption could be misleading. Maybe a claim is made about a new medical treatment based on a research finding—but you're not certain if the cited research paper really said that."

Even more fundamental than teaching the SIFT model, Caulfield said, is the idea that "you're not trying to stop them from sharing bad stuff—you're trying to help them share (and read) *better* stuff." He added, "Simply going at it in a negative way is doomed to fail, because ultimately [they're] sharing for a reason."

Regardless of perceptions, Caulfield explained, the issue is much bigger than just seniors. Even worse is people with power and influence who are being tricked, because they are capable of causing more damage:

> If your dad gets duped it's an awkward Thanksgiving. If your Senator gets duped, thousands of people can die. Hundreds of thousands. Maybe millions, especially when we look at disinformation around climate. I think we really need a broad educational push—I'm suspicious of any push solely around seniors—and I think seniors would be too.

Caulfield is absolutely right. This issue is bigger than just one demographic, which is exactly why it requires a broad educational approach.

Encourage Questioning

Of all the pieces of advice to give to loved ones who share fake news, there is perhaps none more simple, effective, and ancient than this: *ask questions*. If someone truly masters the process of questioning, they will find themselves further and further away from being tricked by *any* claim because they will continue to follow every thread. Upon reading a piece online, it might help to ask why the reporter felt the need to write it, who contributed to the reporting, what industries may have a stake in the questions being raised, whether there are any conflicts of interest, why the story was published when it was, and more. On your way to answering some of these questions, there's a good chance that—if you're reading a piece of fake news—you'll come across more red flags.

Asking questions has been important in philosophy and science for as long as those institutions have existed. Consider the *Socratic method*, for example, a form of questioning developed by Socrates. This wasn't to determine fake news online, obviously, but it *was* created to help seek truth in daily conversations with other people. By learning how to ask important queries, and then probing further in order to see how the answers would actually play out in the real world, anyone can become better at recognizing misinformation.

It's important to acknowledge that some people claim to be asking questions when they are, in fact, making real claims. Some individuals with conspiratorial tendencies, for example, might use this flawed system. Here's how it goes:

Person 1: "Don't you think 9/11 was an inside job? I'm not saying George Bush personally flew the planes into the towers, but there are important questions that need to be answered."

Person 2: "Everything I've looked into has shown that it was outside sources who wanted to hurt us."

Person 1: "Well, are you so gullible that you believe the government would never do us any harm?"

Person 2: "I never said that, but I just haven't seen evidence to prove the attack was an inside job."

Person 1: "Isn't it at least possible that it happened the way I said it did? I'm just asking important questions. You need to do your own research!"

So, asking questions is incredibly important, but it's also crucial not to get stuck in a scenario in which "questions" are actually assertions. In order to truly benefit from asking questions, they have to be sincere and legitimate. Otherwise you're just spinning your wheels, talking for the benefit of hearing yourself talk.

One important question *everyone* should ask when reading the news is, "How old is this?"

Old News

One of the easiest ways to help your friends and family who consistently spread misinformation doesn't require a comprehensive reform to education, or a confrontation, or even an ideological switch. It's to teach them something incredibly simple that most journalists know instinctively: check the date.

When your business is news, every time you look at an article your eye is drawn to a few things, the first of which is almost always the date of its publication. The reason for that is simple: the date tells us if it's *news* or . . . *olds*? It tells a journalist if it's old news—something that's worth absolutely nothing and you can disregard—or new news worth looking at and potentially reporting.

This policy can apply to basically everyone who just wants to make sure they are sharing high-quality items. If you see a piece of news that you want to share, double-check to see that what you're sharing is actually relevant. In some cases, it could be several years old, and simply circulating again because of some other item in the news.

Checking the date on the news articles that you read isn't all that difficult; nor is it a novel piece of advice. In fact, in 2014, the *Columbia Journalism Review* covered the issue of "when old stories go viral" in a story by Ben Adler. As an example of how this phenomenon actually affected someone in the real world, Adler told a story of when people were sharing an article about thirty inches of snow coming up that weekend. The article was old, but that didn't stop people from panicking about the potential for canceled flights (Adler, 2014):

> Stories going viral on social media long after their publication date, as readers mistakenly assume they break fresh news, has become remarkably common. Friends email, tweet, and post

on Facebook stories that came out years before and somehow got revived on social media.

In terms of advice on the subject, Adler says the "onus is on readers to double check the timestamp on things they share," adding:

> In this sort of media environment, where you cannot assume that the link you click on from a major site is actually current, the burden on readers to be careful is increased dramatically. Readers so frequently discover old stories and think they are new that warning them about it has become part of the standard news literacy curriculum.

This is incredibly important. As we discussed above, media literacy is one of the biggest keys toward ending the fake news pandemic. And adding date-verification to that is a simple yet effective way to improve everyone's literacy.

An easy way to help *anyone* with this, including your troubled loved ones, is to teach the popular news literacy mnemonic device: APCs. To "mind your APCs" is to pay attention to the *authority* (does the report come from a respected and educated perspective?), *point-of-view* (is there an agenda or perspective you need to consider?), and *currency* (is this current and relevant?) of a news item (Fleming, 2015).

Unfortunately, even the best advice can fall on deaf ears. It's important to know how to reach people who might seem unreachable.

Closed to Advice?

If someone appears to be closed off to all advice on the issue of fake news, there isn't always something that you can do about it. Due to cognitive dissonance, a culture of stubbornness, a political climate buried to the neck in hyperpartisan narratives, and other factors, you'll probably run into lots of people like this. You can't necessarily reason with someone who has absolutely no intention of even considering other positions, so there will likely be circumstances under which you probably shouldn't waste your time trying to help someone overcome their issues.

That being said, the stubbornness of a particular individual doesn't *always* mean there's no hope. It's true that one of the most frequent objections I get when discussing how to help loved ones with a fake news addiction is that they believe most people are too far gone to accept help. And while this is certainly a valid concern, and *could* be true in certain extreme scenarios, it's also important to recognize that not everyone fits into that box. In fact, I think a lot of us can think of a time when we had been certain about something only to be proven wrong later. There's a chance that the person you're trying to help fits into this category instead, and is just waiting to be shown the right way.

If you *do* want to get through to an individual who has no intention of listening to you, you have to keep in mind a few things. For starters, you have to recognize that it *probably isn't going to work*. You have to begin understanding that you likely won't move the needle whatsoever.

After you've accepted your inevitable failure and chosen to continue on this path for some reason, then the next thing to keep in mind is that nothing will happen in one conversation. You will almost certainly have to take an incremental approach, making minor appeals that don't cause serious confrontation. You aren't trying to change their mind; you're trying to plant a seed to make them think.

Conclusion: Doing Our Part

"Unless someone like you cares a whole awful lot,
Nothing is going to get better. It's not."

—Dr. Seuss, writer (in *The Lorax*)

Apathy is one of the biggest obstacles we must overcome in defeating harmful fake news. A lot of people simply don't care if they spread nonsense stories, or what effects doing so might have on other people and society in general, and that situation presents its own challenges. Motivating those individuals can be next to impossible, because they have to understand the importance of the debate itself first. And, unfortunately, people with that mindset make up a big chunk of the population. To make people *care* about truth would take a pretty major shift in how society teaches education and critical thinking.

But even when people *do* care, and want to help, it can be difficult to figure out how to get things done and *actually* fix the problem. There are unlimited reasons why this is no easy task.

Bystander Effect

For starters, I think a lot of individuals believe someone else will handle rapidly spreading misinformation—that it's the responsibility of the government or corporations. This discourages people from being vocal in a way that could help others and improve the level of discourse, too. In a way, I would consider this a form of the *bystander effect*.

If you haven't heard of this phenomenon, it describes the notion that many individuals are less likely to help someone else in an emergency if there are people around, presumably because they believe others *will* help the person. In some cases, fear is also a factor. If you've ever heard anything suspicious in your neighborhood, but decided to leave it to someone else to handle, then that person could be a victim of the bystander effect.

The most popular story that demonstrates this effect is that of Kitty Genovese, who was reportedly stabbed to death near her home while witnesses watched and listened from their apartments above the street. While the bystander effect has been established using peer-reviewed data, I wouldn't be doing my job as a fighter of fake news if I didn't mention that the details surrounding that story have been called into question in recent years (Benderly, 2012). In fact, the *New York Times*, which itself is responsible for much of the early coverage of Genovese's story, has acknowledged that a number of reported facts, such as the number of witnesses, were exaggerated (Dunlap, 2016).

But none of that puts into jeopardy the psychological research, nor does it invalidate the overall point of the story: that it's important to stand up to help where possible, and not let fear or unwarranted assumptions get in the way of that. And this can be applied to online discussions as well. It's important to fight the apathy, or the self-justification leading you toward inaction, because confronting misinformation is the best way to fight it and make a difference, especially online, where there are observers who might be on the fence about the issue you are discussing. After all, even if you are confronting a serial fake-news offender who has no interest in the truth, there could be *someone* who's listening. This is supported by scientific studies as well. One group of researchers looking into vaccine misinformation recommended confronting fake news in its tracks for exactly this reason (Steffens, Dunn, Wiley, & Leask, 2019):

> We recommend that communicators consider directly countering misinformation because of the potential influence on their silent audience, i.e. those observing but not openly commenting, liking or sharing posts.

Whether others are listening in or not, though, evidence suggests fact-checking in real time can help people. As author Oche Otorkpa has said, "Fake news is like ice, once it comes in contact with the heat of the truth it melts quickly and suddenly evaporates." While this is certainly an oversimplification, considering the factors we talked about earlier, it's a good way to remember that—for some people—fact-checking works.

This is all good advice to anyone hoping to confront fake news online, but what are the best ways to make real change on a grander scale?

Best Practices

That same study mentioned above had additional advice for provaccine activists that can be applied to anyone fighting misinformation. It recommended keeping responses brief, polite, and focused on debunking the fake news. Further, the study suggested there would be benefits to focusing on specific people, those who aren't necessarily activists but appear amenable to new information.

Interestingly, the researchers recommended "pairing scientific evidence with story-telling" in order to make a bigger impact. On its own, the study says, concrete scientific information "is not always sufficient." The researchers wrote:

> [E]xperimental studies suggest narrative forms may be more convincing, a point not lost on anti-vaccine activists. . . . Anecdotes from people personally affected by vaccine-preventable diseases are perceived as particularly credible, although require care in their use given the variable effects of appeals to fear on different audiences. Communicators should bear in mind the narrative structure of their stories, developing specific components such as setting, characters, plot and moral to speak to audience beliefs and values.

On one level, this theory makes a lot of sense. After all, anti-science activists seem to rely primarily on stories, and it appears to be effective on a large segment of the population. So, mixing in some anecdotes could actually be a pretty good move. That being said, there may be some contradiction between this paper and a 2019 study focusing on cervical cancer prevention (Zhang, et al., 2019). In that case, researchers found that clearly presented scientific data was more effective on social media than patients' personal accounts:

> [T]he experimental study revealed that informational tweets were shared significantly more than personal experience tweets; and organizational senders were shared significantly more than individual senders. While rare personal experience messages can achieve large success, they are generally unsuccessful.

It's also important to discuss the limitations of confronting and debunking online fake news directly. Researchers have found, for instance, that sometimes trying to disprove a false statement in the world of politics can actually make things worse. This is called the *quicksand effect*, according to a report from *MIT Technology Review*.

Adam Berinsky, the Mitsui Professor of Political Science at MIT and director of the MIT Political Experiments Research Lab (PERL), said he observed this in 2009 when Republicans were claiming that Barack Obama's idea for the Affordable Care Act contained so-called death panels for the elderly. The *MIT Technology Review* states:

> In reality, the program allowed doctors to inform patients about their end-of-life care options. But as Berinsky found, having Democratic Party figures or even neutral parties attempt to debunk the lie made more people believe it.

No matter how good you are at following these practices, there's always a chance that you'll need some extra help. Here are some resources in case that happens.

Some Helpful Resources

News Literacy Project: The News Literacy Project is a nonprofit organization that provides nonpartisan programs to educate students and young people about how to know quality news from bunk in the digital age. NLP helps educators teach kids how to be smart news consumers and informed members of our democracy, according to its mission statement. The site is here: https://newslit.org/about/

Reveal News: Reveal News, from the Center for Investigative Reporting, has a helpful guide to spotting misinformation. Focusing on corruption news, the nonprofit works with news outlets and conducts in-depth investigations that have won several awards. The guide is here: https://www.revealnews.org/about-us/reveals-guide-to-spotting-fake-news/

UCF Libraries: University of Central Florida has a fake news and fact-checking site that includes definitions, book recommendations, quotes, videos, fact-checking, statistical data, and more. The comprehensive site also informs readers about satirical news sites and commonly misattributed quotes. The site is right here: https://guides.ucf.edu/fakenews

Cornell University Library: Cornell University provides a handy site for evaluating news and recognizing misinformation, complete with definitions and infographics. Their reference guide includes how to see our own biases, how to challenge ideas respectfully, and more. Cornell University's "fake news" guide is here: https://guides.library.cornell.edu/evaluate_news

University of Michigan Library: The University of Michigan Library provides a series of "research guides," including one on news sources. That guide provides tips on international and historical news sources, as well as on "fake news" and misinformation. The link is here: https://guides.lib.umich.edu/news

New York Times Lesson Plan: Two years after the *New York Times* launched its first lesson plan on "fake news" issues in 2015, the paper released its renewed version, "Evaluating Sources in a 'Post-Truth' World: Ideas for Teaching and Learning About Fake News." The program includes several examples of fake news items, and details on how that particular misinformation evolved. The link is here: https://www.nytimes.com/2017/01/19/learning/lesson-plans/evaluating-sources-in-a-post-truth-world-ideas-for-teaching-and-learning-about-fake-news.html

Teaching Kids News: Teaching Kids News was created to help children read and comprehend the news by providing recent developments in kid-friendly language they understand. In addition to producing articles for kids, the group has a comprehensive "fake news" guide with resources. Here's a link to that: https://teachingkidsnews.com/fakenews/

Mount Allison University Libraries: Mount Allison University, in Canada, hosts its own "fake news" guide in its libraries and archives. The site includes tips and resources, including lists of known fake news sites and a guide to "recognizing good journalism." You can access that site here: https://libraryguides.mta.ca/fake_news

These are some helpful and reliable groups with information that will help anyone better understand news media, but, in the end, resources like these are only as effective as the people who make good use of them.

In fact, before anything in this book can be helpful, we need to first accept a few things. We need to understand that "fake news"—or intentional misinformation or click-based junk or whatever you want to call it—can be a big problem in our society. And it doesn't *just* affect those who regularly consume it. Because the stories spread to even the most powerful participants in our political system, the problem affects us all.

In the end, there will be no *one* silver bullet that will stop the spread of dangerous fake news or its impacts on society. Instead, we will need a whole box of silver bullets, including comprehensive media literacy, restoration of faith in journalism, and safeguards for social media. We will need to utilize a variety of methods that preserve the nature of free speech as well as freedom of the press, all while *fighting fake news* in a way that keeps it possible for us to have an informed public capable of making good decisions. We have to dedicate ourselves to researching what we read, and to sharing only quality news. It won't be an easy task, but it's definitely doable if we all work together, regardless of our political differences.

References

Adams, P. (2019, October 17). Don't let ABC's mistake fuel distrust of the media. Poynter. Retrieved from https://www.poynter.org/ethics-trust/2019/dont-let-abcs-mistake-fuel-distrust-of-the-media/

Adler, B. (2014, February 17). When old stories go viral. *Columbia Journalism Review.* Retrieved from https://archives.cjr.org/news_literacy/old_stories_going_viral.php

Adl-Tabatabai, S. (2016, November 24). Fake news 'epidemic' turn out to be false. *NewsPunch.* Retrieved from https://newspunch.com/fake-news-epidemic-turn-out-to-be-false/

All Things Considered. (2016, November 23). We tracked down a fake-news creator in the suburbs. Here's what we learned. *NPR.* Retrieved from: https://www.npr.org/sections/alltechconsidered/2016/11/23/503146770/npr-finds-the-head-of-a-covert-fake-news-operation-in-the-suburbs

Allcott, H., & Gentzkow, M. (2017). Social media and fake news in the 2016 Election. *Journal of Economic Perspectives*, 211–236.

Anand, B. N. (2017, January 5). The U.S. media's problems are much bigger than fake news and filter bubbles. *Harvard Business Review.* Retrieved from https://hbr.org/2017/01/the-u-s-medias-problems-are-much-bigger-than-fake-news-and-filter-bubbles

Armstrong, P. W., & Naylor, C. D. (2019). Counteracting health misinformation. *The Journal of the American Medical Association*, 1863–1864.

Associated Press. (2019, November 6). Report: fake political news and 'misinformation' on Facebook is on the rise. *Time*. Retrieved from https://time.com/5719829/fake-stories-facebook-rise/

Babich, T. (2016, September 26). Anti-vaccine mom changes stance after kids become severely ill. *ABC 7 Chicago*. Retrieved from https://abc7chicago.com/health/anti-vaccine-mom-changes-stance-after-kids-become-severely-ill/1527110/

Banjo, S., & Lung, N. (2019, November 11). How fake news and rumors are stoking division in Hong Kong. *Bloomberg*. Retrieved from https://www.bloomberg.com/news/articles/2019-11-11/how-fake-news-is-stoking-violence-and-anger-in-hong-kong

BBC. (2018, January 1). Germany starts enforcing hate speech law. *BBC News*. Retrieved from https://www.bbc.com/news/technology-42510868

Beauchamp, Z. (2019, July 31). Marianne Williamson isn't funny. She's scary. *Vox*. Retrieved from https://www.vox.com/policy-and-politics/2019/7/31/20748594/marianne-williamson-debate-democratic-july-2019-depression

Beaujon, A. (2019, October 2). Trump claims he invented the term "fake news"—here's an interview with the guy who actually helped popularize it. *Washingtonian*. Retrieved from https://www.washingtonian.com/2019/10/02/trump-claims-he-invented-the-term-fake-news-an-interview-with-the-guy-who-actually-helped-popularize-it/

Beavers, D. (2019, May 19). Gabbard calls unflattering report 'fake news'. *Politico*. Retrieved from https://www.politico.com/story/2019/05/19/tulsi-gabbard-fake-news-1332880

Beiser, E. (2019, December 11). China, Turkey, Saudi Arabia, Egypt are world's worst jailers of journalists. Committee to Protect Journalists. Retrieved from https://cpj.org/reports/2019/12/journalists-jailed-china-turkey-saudi-arabia-egypt.php

Belluz, J. (2018a, May 4). Dr. Oz is a quack. Now Trump's appointing him to be a health adviser. *Vox*. Retrieved from https://www.vox.

com/2018/5/4/17318932/dr-oz-trump-council-sports-fitness-nutrition

Belluz, J. (2018b, September 6). Goop was fined $145,000 for its claims about jade eggs for vaginas. It's still selling them. *Vox*. Retrieved from https://www.vox.com/2018/9/6/17826924/goop-yoni-egg-gwyneth-paltrow-settlement

Benderly, B. L. (2012, September). Psychology's tall tales. American Psychological Association. Retrieved from https://www.apa.org/gradpsych/2012/09/tall-tales

Bergen, M. (2019, November 20). Google limits political ad targeting, bans misleading info. Bloomberg. Retrieved from https://www.bloomberg.com/news/articles/2019-11-20/google-limits-political-ad-targeting-prohibits-misleading-info

Best, J. (2018, February 12). Recognizing 'fake news': media literacy forum aims for more educated electorate. *Santa Maria Times*. Retrieved from https://santamariatimes.com/news/local/recognizing-fake-news-media-literacy-forum-aims-for-more-educated/article_4515bf3f-d679-5108-aa28-585fe9f97d2e.html

Bort, J. (2016, November 14). It took only 36 hours for these students to solve Facebook's fake-news problem. Business Insider. Retrieved from https://www.businessinsider.com/students-solve-facebooks-fake-news-problem-in-36-hours-2016-11

Braun, J. A., & Eklund, J. L. (2019). Fake news, real money: ad tech platforms, profit-driven hoaxes, and the business of journalism. *Digital Journalism*, 1–21.

Breland, A. (2019, November 14). Steve King mixed up his Soros and his whistleblower conspiracy theories. *Mother Jones*. Retrieved from https://www.motherjones.com/politics/2019/11/steve-king-alex-soros/

Briand, X. (2009, July 30). Alternative medicine a big business in U.S.: report. Reuters. Retrieved from https://www.reuters.com/article/us-usa-health-alternative/alternative-medicine-a-big-business-in-u-s-report-idUSTRE56T6MN20090730

Brodesser-Akner, T. (2018, July 25). How Goop's haters made Gwyneth Paltrow's company worth $250 million. *New York Times*. Retrieved from https://www.nytimes.com/2018/07/25/magazine/big-business-gwyneth-paltrow-wellness.html

Cambridge University Press. (n.d.). Fake news. Cambridge University. Retrieved from https://dictionary.cambridge.org/us/dictionary/english/fake-news

Cao, J., Galinsky, A. D., & Maddux, W. W. (2013). Does travel broaden the mind? Breadth of foreign experiences increases generalized trust. *Social Psychological and Personality Science.*

Carol Tavris, E. A. (2009). *Mistakes were made (but not by me): why we justify foolish beliefs, bad decisions, and hurtful acts.* Mariner Books.

Carr, D. (2012, July 8). The fissures are growing for papers. *New York Times.* Retrieved from https://nyti.ms/3igRLfw

Carroll, A. E. (2019, July 22). Health facts aren't enough. Should persuasion become a priority? *New York Times.* Retrieved from https://www.nytimes.com/2019/07/22/upshot/health-facts-importance-persuasion.html

Caulfield, M. (2019, June 19). SIFT (the four moves). Hapgood. Retrieved from https://hapgood.us/2019/06/19/sift-the-four-moves/

CBS News. (2016, October 21). Family hopes Playboy model's death brings awareness to chiropractic risks. *CBS This Morning.* Retrieved from https://www.cbsnews.com/news/katie-may-playboy-model-death-stroke-after-chiropractor-visit-family-speaks-out/

CBS News. (n.d.). Infowars. Don't get fooled by these fake news sites. *CBS News.* Retrieved from https://www.cbsnews.com/pictures/dont-get-fooled-by-these-fake-news-sites/4/

Center for Information Technology & Society. (n.d.). The danger of fake news in inflaming or suppressing social conflict. UCSB CITS. Retrieved from https://cits.ucsb.edu/fake-news/danger-social

Chahal, M. (2017, March 27). The fake news effect: What does it mean for advertisers? *MarketingWeek.* Retrieved from https://www.marketingweek.com/the-fake-news-effect/

Christopher A. Bail, L. P. (2018). Exposure to opposing views on social media can increase political polarization. *Proceedings of the National Academy of Sciences of the United States of America (PNAS),* 1–6.

Chung, S.-H. (2018). How does cognitive dissonance influence the sunk cost effect? *Psychology Research and Behavior Management*, 37–45.

Clarke, J. S., Leach, A., & van der Zee, B. (2015, February 18). Easily distracted but vital; what NGOs really think about journalists. *Guardian*. Retrieved from https://www.theguardian.com/global-development-professionals-network/2015/feb/18/ngos-journalists-media-development-communications

Coen, S. (2018, August 28). Facebook has introduced a user trustworthiness score—here's why it should go further. Phys.org. Retrieved from https://phys.org/news/2018-08-facebook-user-trustworthiness-score.html

Collins, D. (2018, August 1). If Silicon Valley won't stop fake news, we will. *Guardian*. Retrieved from https://www.theguardian.com/commentisfree/2018/aug/01/big-tech-control-politics-fake-news-data-facebook-ads-elections

Couldry, N., & Turow, J. (2014). Advertising, big data and the clearance of the public realm: marketers' new approaches to the content subsidy. *International Journal of Communication*, 1710–1726.

Dastagir, A. E. (2019, March 8). Facts alone don't sway anti-vaxxers. So what does? *USA Today*. Retrieved from https://www.usatoday.com/story/news/investigations/2019/03/08/vaccine-anti-vax-anti-vaxxer-what-change-their-mind-vaccine-hesitancy/3100216002/

Dewey, C. (2016, June 16). 6 in 10 of you will share this link without reading it, a new, depressing study says. *Washington Post*. Retrieved from https://www.washingtonpost.com/news/the-intersect/wp/2016/06/16/six-in-10-of-you-will-share-this-link-without-reading-it-according-to-a-new-and-depressing-study/

Dictionary.com. (n.d.). Fake news. Dictionary.com. Retrieved from https://www.dictionary.com/browse/fake-news

Dictionary.com. (n.d.). Freedom of speech. Dictionary.com. Retrieved from https://www.dictionary.com/browse/freedom-of-speech?s=t

Oxford Living Dictionaries. (n.d.). Disinformation. Oxford Living Dictionaries. Retrieved from https://en.oxforddictionaries.com/definition/disinformation

Dolan, E. W. (2013, December 9). New study confirms Mark Twain's saying: travel is fatal to prejudice. Psypost.org. Retrieved from https://www.psypost.org/2013/12/new-study-confirms-mark-twains-saying-travel-is-fatal-to-prejudice-21662

Donsbach, W. (1991). Exposure to political content in newspapers: the impact of cognitive dissonance on readers' selectivity. *European Journal of Communication*.

Dorroh, J. (2019, November 8). Serbian journalist: undermining the media is first step in dismantling democracy. International Center for Journalists. Retrieved from https://www.icfj.org/news/serbian-journalist-undermining-media-first-step-dismantling-democracy

Dunlap, D. W. (2016, April 6). 1964 | How many witnessed the murder of Kitty Genovese? *New York Times*. Retrieved from https://www.nytimes.com/2016/04/06/insider/1964-how-many-witnessed-the-murder-of-kitty-genovese.html

Dunlop, R., & Ryan, J. (2017, December 11). A Kentucky preacher-turned-politician's web of lies. The Pope's Long Con. Retrieved from http://longcon.kycir.org/

Dye, A. (2019, September 16). AP's transphobic Sam Smith story exposes journalism's failings. *Tampa Bay Times*. Retrieved from https://www.tampabay.com/opinion/2019/09/16/aps-transphobic-sam-smith-story-exposes-journalisms-failings-ashley-dye/

Edmonson, G. (2012, June 22). Wall Street Journal makes numerous, uncorrected mistakes on editorial pages. Poynter. Retrieved from https://www.poynter.org/reporting-editing/2012/wall-street-journal-makes-numerous-uncorrected-mistakes-on-editorial-pages/

Ernst, E. (2010). Deaths after chiropractic: a review of published cases. *International Journal of Clinical Practice*, 1162–1165.

Facebook. (2018, August 6). Enforcing out community standards. Facebook Newsroom. Retrieved from https://newsroom.fb.com/news/2018/08/enforcing-our-community-standards/

Faiola, A., & Kirchner, S. (2017, April 5). How do you stop fake news? In Germany, with a law. Washington Post. Retrieved from https://www.washingtonpost.com/world/europe/how-do-you-stop-fake-news-in-germany-with-a-law/2017/04/05/e6834ad6-1a08-11e7-bcc2-7d1a0973e7b2_story.html

Jessie Ball duPont Library. (2019, July 26). Fake news. Jessie Ball du-Pont Library. Retrieved from https://library.sewanee.edu/fakenews

Farrington, D. (2016, May 13). Trump denies posing as his own spokesman, rebuts audio recording. NPR. Retrieved from https://www.npr.org/sections/thetwo-way/2016/05/13/477939211/trump-denies-posing-as-his-own-spokesman-refutes-audio-recording

Fazio, L. K., Payne, B. K., Brashier, N. M., & Marsh, E. J. (2015). Knowledge does not protect against illusory truth. *Journal of Experimental Psychology*, 993–1002.

FDA. (2009, May). FDA 101: health fraud awareness. FDA Consumer Health Information. Retrieved from https://www.fda.gov/media/77211/download

FDA. (2010, October 1). 'Miracle' treatment turns into potent bleach. U.S. Food & Drug Administration. Retrieved from https://wayback.archive-it.org/7993/20170111070843/http:/www.fda.gov/ForConsumers/ConsumerUpdates/ucm228052.htm

Feldscher, K. (2019, April 24). Steve King says he relates to what Christ 'went through for us' after controversies. CNN. Retrieved from https://www.cnn.com/2019/04/24/politics/steve-king-jesus-christ/index.html?fbclid=IwAR38r6lz0wLO9of8kCQMZx0XvEsvdw27QSpHSnPkYckEg30I0M6ioqvaoc4

Feldstein, M. (2016). Watergate revisited. *American Journailsm Review*, 1–9.

Fernbach, P. M., Light, N., Scott, S. E., Inbar, Y., & Rozin, P. (2019). Extreme opponents of genetically modified foods know the least but think they know the most. *Nature Human Behaviour*, 251–256.

Filipsson, A. F. (1996). Short term inhalation exposure to turpentine: toxicokinetics and acute effects in men. *Occupational and Environmental Medicine*, 100–105.

Fleming, J. (2015). What do facts have to do with it? Exploring instructional emphasis. *Journal of Media Literacy Education*, 73–92.

Friedlander, E. (2019, May 11). Why people post fake news. Vice. Retrieved from https://www.vice.com/en_us/article/9kpz3v/why-people-post-fake-news-v26n1

Gabielkov, M., Ramachandran, A., Chaintreau, A., & Legout, A. (2016). Social clicks: what and who gets read on Twitter? ACM Sigmetrics.

Gander, K. (2019, October 31). Vaxxed 2 tickets: anti-vaccine documentary sequel to secretly screen in 19 states to try and avoid being blocked. *Newsweek*. Retrieved from https://www.newsweek.com/vaxxed-2-tickets-anti-vaccine-documentary-sequel-secret-blocked-1468899

Gartman, E. (n.d.). Nazi war crimes trials: interview with the devil: a Holocaust survivor interviews a death camp supervisor. Jewish Virtual Library. Retrieved from https://www.jewishvirtual-library.org/interview-with-the-devil-a-holocaust-survivor-interviews-a-death-camp-supervisor

Gesley, J. (2019, August 20). Germany: Facebook found in violation of "anti-fake news" law. *Global Legal Monitor*. Retrieved from https://www.loc.gov/law/foreign-news/article/germany-facebook-found-in-violation-of-anti-fake-news-law/

Good Day Sacramento. (2018, September 27). Governor Brown vetoes fake news advisory group bill, calls it 'not necessary'. *CBS13*. Retrieved from https://gooddaysacramento.cbslocal.com/2018/09/27/california-fake-news-bill-veto/

Gorski, D. (2012, November 11). Reiki invades an operating room. Science Blogs. Retrieved from https://scienceblogs.com/insolence/2012/11/12/reiki-invades-an-operating-room

Graham, M. (2019, November 12). Ahead of the 2020 election, this Israeli start-up is using military-grade tech to fight fake news. *CNBC*. Retrieved from https://www.cnbc.com/2019/11/12/israeli-start-up-cheq-is-using-military-grade-tech-to-fight-fake-news.html

Grandoni, D. (2012, February 6). Congressman falls for the Onion's Planned Parenthood 'abortionplex' story. *Atlantic*. Retrieved from https://www.theatlantic.com/national/archive/2012/02/congressman-falls-months-old-onion-story-about-planned-parenthood-abortionplex/332189/

Grimes, D. R. (2016, November 8). Impartial journalism is laudable. But false balance is dangerous. *Guardian*. Retrieved from https://www.theguardian.com/science/blog/2016/nov/08/impartial-journalism-is-laudable-but-false-balance-is-dangerous

Grimes, D. R. (2017, May 15). 'Outlandish therapies' exploit families of autistic children. *Irish Times*. Retrieved from https://www.irishtimes.com/life-and-style/health-family/outlandish-therapies-exploit-families-of-autistic-children-1.3076647

Guess, A., Nagler, J., & Tucker, J. (2019). Less than you think: prevalence and predictors of fake news dissemination on Facebook. *Science Advances*.

Gunter, J. (2018, August 1). Worshiping the false idols of wellness. *New York Times*. Retrieved from https://www.nytimes.com/2018/08/01/style/wellness-industrial-complex.html?smid=tw-nytstyles&smtyp=cur

Gunther, R., Beck, P. A., & Nisbet, E. C. (2018). *Fake news may have contributed to Trump's 2016 victory*. Columbus: Ohio State University.

Ha, A. (2019, May 17). Credder offers Rotten Tomatoes–style ratings for the news. Tech Crunch. Retrieved from https://techcrunch.com/2019/05/17/credder-offers-rotten-tomatoes-style-ratings-for-the-news/

Harari, Y. N. (2018, August 5). Yuval Noah Harari extract: 'humans are a post-truth species'. *Guardian*. Retrieved from https://www.theguardian.com/culture/2018/aug/05/yuval-noah-harari-extract-fake-news-sapiens-homo-deus

Harrison, G. P. (2019, July 18). How to keep fake news out of your head. *Psychology Today*. Retrieved from https://www.psychologytoday.com/us/blog/about-thinking/201907/how-keep-fake-news-out-your-head

Harvard Medical School. (2011, July). How addiction hijacks the brain. Harvard Health Publishing. Retrieved from https://www.health.harvard.edu/newsletter_article/how-addiction-hijacks-the-brain

Helman, C. (2013, January 21). Breaking: a local newspaper chain that's actually making good money. *Forbes*. Retrieved from https://

www.forbes.com/sites/christopherhelman/2013/01/02/new-shoots-in-old-growth/#5b9d7bc78dc2

Henkel, I. (2018). How the laughing, irreverent Briton trumped fact-checking: a textual analysis of fake news in British newspaper stories about the EU. *Journalism Education*, 87–97.

Herbert, G. (2017, February 16). David Muir talks 'fake news,' Trump in interview with Jimmy Kimmel [video]. Syracuse.com. Retrieved from https://www.syracuse.com/tv/2017/02/david_muir_fake_news_trump_jimmy_kimmel.html

Hern, A. (2017, March 6). Google accused of spreading fake news. *Guardian*. Retrieved from https://www.theguardian.com/technology/2017/mar/06/google-accused-spreading-fake-news

Hiltzik, M. (2015, April 24). Dr. Oz fires back at his critics—with misdirection and an absurd defense. *Los Angeles Times*. Retrieved from https://www.latimes.com/business/hiltzik/la-fi-mh-dr-oz-defense-im-a-doctor-20150423-column.html

Hindman, M., & Barash, V. (2018). *Disinformation, 'fake news' and influence campaigns on Twitter*. Miami: October.

Harvard Health Publishing. (2011, July). How addiction hijacks the brain. Retrieved from https://www.health.harvard.edu/newsletter_article/how-addiction-hijacks-the-brain

Huberman, B. (2019, July 9). 'Fake news': why Snopes prefers not to say it anymore. Snopes. Retrieved from https://www.snopes.com/2019/07/09/fake-news-why-snopes-prefers-not-to-say-it-anymore/

Izuma, K. (n.d.). What happens to the brain during cognitive dissonance? *Scientific American*. Retrieved from https://www.scientificamerican.com/article/what-happens-to-the-brain-during-cognitive-dissonance1/

Jensen, E. (2019, July 16). After infamous R. Kelly sit-down, Gayle King isn't surprised by his arrest. *USA Today*. Retrieved from https://www.usatoday.com/story/entertainment/celebrities/2019/07/16/r-kelly-charges-gayle-king-says-new-indictments-not-surprise/1742255001/

Kang, C., & Goldman, A. (2016, December 5). In Washington pizzeria attack, fake news brought real guns. *New York Times*. Retrieved from https://www.mediapicking.com/medias/files_medias/in-washington-pizzeria-attack--fake-news-brought-real-guns---the-new-york-times-0733795001481729212.pdf

Kent, T. (2018, September 6). Fake news is about to get so much more dangerous. *Washington Post*. Retrieved from https://www.washingtonpost.com/opinions/fake-news-is-about-to-get-so-much-more-dangerous/2018/09/06/3d7e4194-a1a6-11e8-83d2-70203b8d7b44_story.html

Khazan, O. (2017, February 2). Why fake news targeted Trump supporters. *Atlantic*. Retrieved from https://www.theatlantic.com/science/archive/2017/02/why-fake-news-targeted-trump-supporters/515433/

Kirtley, J. E. (n.d.). Getting to the Truth: fake news, libel laws, and "enemies of the American people". *Human Rights Magazine*. Retrieved from https://www.americanbar.org/groups/crsj/publications/human_rights_magazine_home/the-ongoing-challenge-to-define-free-speech/getting-to-the-truth/

Klein, J. (2016, March 10). The media came too late to the promise of John Kasich. *Time*. Retrieved from https://time.com/4253732/distracted-by-trump-we-the-media-came-too-late-to-the-promise-of-john-kasich/

Knight Foundation. (2018). Indicators of news media trust. Gallup/Knight Foundation .

Kopf, D. (2017, January 29). A new study kills the notion that fake news swung the US election to Trump. Quartz. Retrieved from https://qz.com/896758/a-new-study-kills-the-notion-that-fake-news-swung-the-us-election-to-trump/

Korownyk, C., Kolber, M. R., McCormack, J., Lam, V., Overbo, K., Cotton, C., . . . Allan, G. M. (2014). Televised medical talk shows—what they recommend and the evidence to support their recommendations: a prospective observational study. *BMJ*.

Lannom, P. (2019, March 28). 'Hinsdale school news' is no such thing. *Hinsdalean*, 3.

Lazer, D. M., Baum, M. A., Benkler, Y., Berinsky, A. J., Greenhill, M.

K., Menczer, F., . . . Zittrain, J. L. (2018). The science of fake news. *Science*, 359(6380), 1094–1096. doi:10.1126/science.aao2998

Lee, B. Y. (2018, August 16). Alex Jones' top 10 health claims and why they are wrong. *Forbes*. Retrieved from https://www.forbes.com/sites/brucelee/2018/08/16/alex-jones-top-10-health-claims-and-why-they-are-wrong/#123b277c3e7f

Lennon, A. (2019, June 4). Could taxes deter the spread of harmful fake news? *BU Today*. Retrieved from https://www.bu.edu/articles/2019/could-taxes-deter-spread-of-fake-news

Lewis, T. (2015, April 24). More than 1,000 doctors say Dr. Oz should resign. Live Science. Retrieved from https://www.livescience.com/50621-dr-oz-should-resign-poll.html

Little-Saña, A. (2018, June 27). How do we know what's true anymore? League of Women Voters of the US (LWVUS). Retrieved from https://www.lwv.org/blog/how-do-we-know-whats-true-anymore

Mack, D. (2019, August 21). Rick Perry, the man in charge of American nuclear weapons, fell for an Instagram hoax. BuzzFeed News. Retrieved from https://www.buzzfeednews.com/article/davidmack/rick-perry-instagram-hoax-meme

Manson, J. E., & Bassuk, S. S. (2018). Vitamin and mineral supplements: what clinicians need to know. *JAMA*, 859–860.

Markel, D. H. (2018, May 5). How Nellie Bly went undercover to expose abuse of the mentally ill. *PBS*. Retrieved from https://www.pbs.org/newshour/nation/how-nellie-bly-went-undercover-to-expose-abuse-of-the-mentally-ill

Martens, B., Aguiar, L., Gomez-Herrera, E., & Mueller-Langer, F. (2018). The digital transformation of news media and the rise of disinformation and fake news. Joint Research Centre.

Martin, E. (2019, February 19). Here's the budget breakdown of a 37-year-old ex-CIA analyst turned energy healer who makes $108,000 a year. *CNBC*. Retrieved from https://www.cnbc.com/2019/02/19/budget-breakdown-of-a-37-year-old-who-makes-108000-dollars-a-year.html

Martínez, M. (2018, November 12). Burned to death because of a rumour on WhatsApp. *BBC News*. Retrieved from https://www.bbc.com/news/world-latin-america-46145986

McAfee, D. (2017, October 20). These people think drinking turpentine will cure any disease. No Sacred Cows. Retrieved from https://www.patheos.com/blogs/nosacredcows/2017/10/people-are-drinking-turpentine/

McAfee, D. G. (2017, August 2). The church of Scientology accused me of "anti-religious bigotry"—here's my response. No Sacred Cows. Retrieved from https://www.patheos.com/blogs/nosacredcows/2017/08/church-scientology-accused-anti-religious-bigotry-heres-response/?fbclid=IwAR1MXLkyYuJoZIQFDzL1FgPCOGQ5POH_2I6t9gXXL5HbE4YxPSP3Yeej7mw

McAfee, D. G. (2019, November 11). YouTube bans "harmful treatments" like black salve and bleach drinking. No Sacred Cows. Retrieved from https://www.patheos.com/blogs/nosacredcows/2019/11/youtube-bans-harmful-treatments-like-black-salve-and-bleach-drinking/

McClure, T. (2019, September 17). Dark crystals: the brutal reality behind a booming wellness craze. *Guardian*. Retrieved from https://www.theguardian.com/lifeandstyle/2019/sep/17/healing-crystals-wellness-mining-madagascar

McDonell-Parry, A. (2016, December 28). 5 things we learned from 'Scientology and the aftermath,' episode 5. *Rolling Stone*. Retrieved from https://www.rollingstone.com/tv/tv-news/5-things-we-learned-from-scientology-and-the-aftermath-episode-5-110793/

McDonnell, P. J., & Sanchez, C. (2018, September 21). When fake news kills: lynchings in Mexico are linked to viral child-kidnap rumors. *Los Angeles Times*. Retrieved from https://www.latimes.com/world/la-fg-mexico-vigilantes-20180921-story.html

McIntyre, L. (2019, May 14). Flat Earthers, and the rise of science denial in America. *Newsweek*. Retrieved from https://www.newsweek.com/flat-earth-science-denial-america-1421936

McLaughlin, T. (2018, December 12). How WhatsApp fuels fake news and violence in India. *Wired*. Retrieved from https://www.wired.com/story/how-whatsapp-fuels-fake-news-and-violence-in-india/

Melford, C., & Fagan, C. (2019). *Cutting the funding of disinformation: the ad-tech solution*. London: The Global DIsinformation Index.

Merriam-Webster. (n.d.). Definition of freedom of speech. *Merriam-Webster*. Retrieved from https://www.merriam-webster.com/dictionary/freedom%20of%20speech

Meyer, R. (2017, February 3). The rise of progressive 'fake news'. *Atlantic*. Retrieved from https://www.theatlantic.com/technology/archive/2017/02/viva-la-resistance-content/515532/

Oxford Living Dictionaries. (n.d.). Misinformation. Oxford Living Dictionaries. Retrieved from https://en.oxforddictionaries.com/definition/misinformation

Mitchell, A., Gottfried, J., Stocking, G., Walker, M., & Fedeli, S. (2019, June 5). Many Americans say made-up news is a critical problem that needs to be fixed. Pew Research Center, Journalism & Media. Retrieved from https://www.journalism.org/2019/06/05/many-americans-say-made-up-news-is-a-critical-problem-that-needs-to-be-fixed/

Moore, J. E., & Socolow, M. J. (2018, September 10). Violence against the media isn't new—history shows why it largely disappeared and has now returned. Associated Press.

Moyers, B. (2019, May 22). What if reporters covered the climate crisis like Edward R. Murrow covered the start of World War II? *Columbia Journalism Review*. Retrieved from https://www.cjr.org/watchdog/bill-moyers-climate-change.php

Murphy, G., Loftus, E. F., Hofstein Grady, R., Levine, L. J., & Greene, C. M. (2019). False memories for fake news during Ireland's abortion referendum. *Psychological Science*.

Newton, C. (2019, January 10). The good news about elderly people sharing so much fake news. *The Verge*. Retrieved from https://www.theverge.com/2019/1/10/18176162/fake-news-old-people-nyu-study-silver-lining

Newton, C. (2019b, February 25). The trauma floor. *The Verge*. Retrieved from https://www.theverge.com/2019/2/25/18229714/cognizant-facebook-content-moderator-interviews-trauma-working-conditions-arizona

Nielsen, R. K., & Graves, L. (n.d.). "News you don't believe": audience perspectives on fake news. Reuters Institute for the Study of Journalism.

Nilsson, M. L., & Örnebring, H. (2016, April 15). Journalism under threat: intimidation and harassment of Swedish journalists. *Journalism Practice*, 10(7), 880-890. doi:10.1080/17512786.2016.1164614

O'Brien, N., Latessa, S., Evangelopoulos, G., & Boix, X. (2018). *The language of fake news: opening the black-box of deep learning based detectors*. Cambridge: MIT.

O'Donovan, C. (2019, February 22). YouTube just demonetized anti-vax channels. BuzzFeed News. Retrieved from https://www.buzzfeednews.com/article/carolineodonovan/youtube-just-demonetized-anti-vax-channels

O'Donovan, C., & McDonald, L. (2019, February 20). YouTube continues to promote anti-vax videos as Facebook prepares to fight medical misinformation. BuzzFeed News. Retrieved from https://www.buzzfeednews.com/article/carolineodonovan/youtube-anti-vaccination-video-recommendations

O'Hear, S. (2018). Facebook is buying UK's Bloomsbury AI to ramp up natural language tech in London. Tech Crunch. Retrieved from https://techcrunch.com/2018/07/02/thebloomsbury/

Ohlheiser, A. (2016, November 18). This is how Facebook's fake-news writers make money. *Washington Post*. Retrieved from https://www.washingtonpost.com/news/the-intersect/wp/2016/11/18/this-is-how-the-internets-fake-news-writers-make-money/

Olivola, C. Y. (2018). The interpersonal sunk-cost effect. *Psychological Science*, 1072–1083.

Olshansky, A. (2018). Conspiracy theorizing and religious motivated reasoning: why the Earth 'must' be flat. Texas Tech University.

O'Rourke, A. (2016, September 15). Dr. Oz's net worth reveals he & Donald Trump both live a privileged life. Bustle. Retrieved from https://www.bustle.com/articles/184084-dr-ozs-net-worth-reveals-he-donald-trump-both-live-a-privileged-life

Parkinson, H. J. (2016, November 14). Click and elect: how fake news helped Donald Trump win a real election. *Guardian*. Retrieved from https://www.theguardian.com/commentisfree/2016/nov/14/fake-news-donald-trump-election-alt-right-social-media-tech-companies

Pennycock, G., Cannon, T., & Rand, D. G. (2018). Prior exposure increases perceived accuracy of fake news. *Journal of Experimental Psychology General*.

Pettit, H. (2019, November 12). Jeremy Corbyn 'backs Boris Johnson for prime minister' in eerily realistic deepfake clip. *Sun*. Retrieved from https://www.thesun.co.uk/tech/10328958/jeremy-corbyn-boris-johnson-election-deepfake-clips/

Posetti, J., & Matthews, A. (2018). A short guide to the history of 'fakes news' and disinformation. International Center for Journalists. Retrieved from https://www.icfj.org/news/short-guide-history-fake-news-and-disinformation-new-icfj-learning-module

Pritchard, T. (2018, October 13). This year's 'worst pseudoscience award' goes to anti-vax fraud Andrew Wakefield. Gizmodo UK. Retrieved from https://www.gizmodo.co.uk/2018/10/this-years-worst-pseudoscience-award-goes-to-anti-vax-fraud-andrew-wakefield/

Radio Free Europe/Radio Liberty. (n.d.). About us. Radio Free Europe/Radio Liberty. Retrieved from https://pressroom.rferl.org/about-us

Rat, R. (2019, June 13). Female sport reporters face floods of sexist insults over World Cup coverage. European Centre for Press & Media Freedom. Retrieved from https://www.ecpmf.eu/news/threats/female-sport-reporters-face-floods-of-sexist-insults-over-world-cup-coverage

Reboot Foundation. (n.d.). The real solution to fake news. Reboot. Retrieved from https://reboot-foundation.org/the-real-solution-to-fake-news/#

Reporters without Borders. (2019). RSF index 2019: Institutional attacks on the press in the US and Canada. RSF.

Research News. (2019, January 2). Software that can automatically detect fake news. Fraunhofer. Retrieved from https://www.

fraunhofer.de/en/press/research-news/2019/february/software-that-can-automatically-detect-fake-news.html

Reuters. (2019, November 24). Singapore issues first correction request under "fake news" law. *Reuters*. Retrieved from https://www.reuters.com/article/singapore-fake/singapore-issues-first-correction-request-under-fake-news-law-idUSL4N28514H

Roy, J. (2019, July 10). How millennials replaced religion with astrology and crystals. *Los Angeles Times*. Retrieved from https://www.latimes.com/health/la-he-millennials-religion-zodiac-tarot-crystals-astrology-20190710-story.html

RTDNA. (2018, January 18). Eight journalists enter 2018 facing criminal charges. *RTDNA*. Retrieved from https://www.rtdna.org/article/eight_journalists_enter_2018_facing_criminal_charges

Russell, C. (2010). Covering controversial science: improving reporting on science and public policy. In D. Kennedy, & G. Overholser, *Science and the Media* (p. 13). Cambridge: American Academy of Arts & Sciences.

Rutenberg, J. (2018, October 28). Trump's attacks on the news media are working. *New York Times*. Retrieved from https://www.nytimes.com/2018/10/28/business/media/trumps-attacks-news-media.html

Schein, M. (2018, May 25). Dr. Oz makes millions even though he's been called a 'charlatan' (and you should follow his lead). *Forbes*. Retrieved from https://www.forbes.com/sites/michaelschein/2018/05/25/dr-oz-makes-millions-even-though-hes-a-total-fraud-and-other-reasons-you-should-follow-his-lead/#49fe108e5fe1

Schmidt, C. (2017, August 3). Games might be a good tool for fighting fake news. Here's what three developers have learned. *NiemanLab*. Retrieved from https://www.niemanlab.org/2017/08/games-might-be-a-good-tool-for-fighting-fake-news-heres-what-three-developers-have-learned/

School, H. M. (2011, July). How addiction hijacks the brain. Harvard Health Publishing. Retrieved from https://www.health.harvard.edu/newsletter_article/how-addiction-hijacks-the-brain

Schwartz, A. B. (2015, May 6). The infamous "war of the worlds" radio broadcast was a magnificent fluke. Smithsonian.com. Retrieved from https://www.smithsonianmag.com/history/infamous-war-worlds-radio-broadcast-was-magnificent-fluke-180955180/

Shao, C., Ciampaglia, G. L., Varol, O., Yang, K., Alessandro, F., & Filippo, M. (2018). The spread of low-credibility content. ArXiv, 1–41.

Sherfinski, D. (2019, August 2). Marianne Williamson defends views about antidepressants: 'I'm pro medicine. I'm pro science'. *Washington Times*. Retrieved from https://www.washingtontimes.com/news/2019/aug/2/marianne-williamson-defends-views-about-antidepres/

Silverman, C. (2019, July 23). People in your life are sharing false or extreme content. BuzzFeed News. Retrieved from https://www.buzzfeednews.com/article/craigsilverman/young-people-worry-about-older-people-sharing-fake-news

Silverman, C., & Alexander, L. (2016, November 3). How teens in the Balkans are duping Trump supporters with fake news. BuzzFeed News. Retrieved from https://www.buzzfeednews.com/article/craigsilverman/how-macedonia-became-a-global-hub-for-pro-trump-misinfo#.qjya8vPv4

Singh, A. (2017, November 2). 'Cuffing season' and 'Corbynmania' are named words of the year by Collins Dictionary. *Telegraph*. Retrieved from https://www.telegraph.co.uk/news/2017/11/02/cuffing-season-corbynmania-named-words-year-collins-dictionary/

Snyder, T. (2019, October 16). How Hitler pioneered 'fake news'. *New York Times*. Retrieved from www.nytimes.com/2019/10/16/opinion/hitler-speech-1919.html

Solomon, D. (2019, August 22). Of course Rick Perry fell for the Instagram hoax. *Texas Monthly*. Retrieved from https://www.texasmonthly.com/politics/rick-perry-instagram-hoax/

Spiegel Staff. (2016, 02 24). Germans lose faith in the fourth estate. Spiegel Online. Retrieved from https://www.spiegel.de/international/germany/most-germans-think-the-press-is-lying-to-them-about-refugees-a-1079049.html

Stayt, C. (2018, October 9). Gwyneth Paltrow on Goop: we disagree with pseudoscience claims. BBC. Retrieved from https://www.bbc.com/news/av/entertainment-arts-45794662/gwyneth-paltrow-on-goop-we-disagree-with-pseudoscience-claims

Steffens, M. S., Dunn, A. G., Wiley, K. E., & Leask, J. (2019). How organisations promoting vaccination respond to misinformation on social media: a qualitative investigation. *BMC Public Health*.

Steig, C. (2019, October 29). Gwyneth Paltrow says she made 'grave mistakes' with Goop that cost millions of dollars. CNBC. Retrieved from https://cnb.cx/3a53VVM

Steinebach, M., Gotkowski, K., & Liu, H. (2019). Fake news detection by image montage recognition. 14th International Conference on Availability, Reliability and Security. doi.org/10.1145/3339252.3341487

Stelter, B. (2015, April 21). Dr. Oz to critics: my show and I 'will not be silenced'. *CNN Business*. Retrieved from https://money.cnn.com/2015/04/21/media/dr-mehmet-oz-accusations

Stroud, N. J. (2008). Media use and political predispositions: revisiting. political behavior, 358–359.

Sullivan, M. (2017, January 8). It's time to retire the tainted term 'fake news'. *Washington Post*. Retrieved from https://wapo.st/2DFs0GS

Sydell, L. (2016, November 23). NPR reporter tracked down a fake-news creator; here's what she learned. KQED. Retrieved from https://www.kqed.org/news/11187539/npr-tracked-down-a-fake-news-creator-in-the-suburbs-heres-what-they-learned

Tavernise, S., Harmon, A., & Salam, M. (2018, June 28). 5 people dead in shooting at Maryland's Capital Gazette newsroom. *New York Times*. Retrieved from https://www.nytimes.com/2018/06/28/us/capital-gazette-annapolis-shooting.html

The Editors, CJR. (2017, July 28). Q&A: Louis Theroux on interviewing controversial subjects. *Columbia Journalism Review*. Retrieved from https://www.cjr.org/special_report/qa-louis-theroux-on-interviewing-controversial-subjects.php

The Information Society Project and the Floyd Abrams Institute for Freedom of Expression. (2017). *Fighting fake news: workshop report*.

New Haven: Oscar M. Ruebhausen Fund at Yale Law School.

This Morning. (2019, October 1). Dr Sara investigates . . . the truth behind childhood vaccines. *ITV*. Retrieved from https://www.itv.com/thismorning/health/dr-sara-investigates-the-truth-behind-childhood-vaccines

Thompson, D. (2017, May 4). Donald Trump is helping the very media organizations he despises. *Atlantic*. Retrieved from https://www.theatlantic.com/business/archive/2017/05/donald-trump-media-enemies/525381/

Ungku, F. (2019, April 2). Factbox: 'fake news' laws around the world. Reuters. Retrieved from https://www.reuters.com/article/us-singapore-politics-fakenews-factbox/factbox-fake-news-laws-around-the-world-idUSKCN1RE0XN

United States Courts. (n.d.). What does free speech mean? Judicial Branch of the U.S. Government. Retrieved from https://www.uscourts.gov/about-federal-courts/educational-resources/about-educational-outreach/activity-resources/what-does

United States Holocaust Memorial Museum. (n.d.). Nazy propaganda and censorship. *Holocaust Encyclopedia*. Retrieved from https://encyclopedia.ushmm.org/content/en/article/nazi-propaganda-and-censorship

Uribarri, A. (n.d.). The *Times* and Jayson Blair. Society of Professional Journalists. Retrieved from https://www.spj.org/ecs13.asp

Vosoughi, S., Roy, D., & Aral, S. (2018). The spread of true and false news online. *Science*, 1146–1151.

WDRB. (2017, December 13). Kentucky state rep. Dan Johnson dies of self-inflicted gunshot wound in Mt. Washington. *WDRB*. Retrieved from https://www.wdrb.com/news/kentucky-state-rep-dan-johnson-dies-of-self-inflicted-gunshot/article_fafeb844-09a3-5839-902a-da85dfa3d7e9.html

Wendling, M. (2018, January 22). The (almost) complete history of 'fake news'. *BBC*. Retrieved from https://www.bbc.com/news/blogs-trending-42724320

Westneat, D. (2016, November 18). Seattle's own 'click-bait' news site serves up red meat for liberals. *Seattle Times*. Retrieved from seattletimes.com/seattle-news/seattles-own-click-bait-news-site-serves-up-red-meat-for-liberals/

Winder, D. (2019, October 8). Forget fake news, deepfake videos are really all about non-consensual porn. *Forbes*. Retrieved from https://www.forbes.com/sites/daveywinder/2019/10/08/forget-2020-election-fake-news-deepfake-videos-are-all-about-the-porn/#78437e6763f9

Wischhover, C. (2018, June 15). Goop is categorizing its wellness stories from "rigorously tested" to "for your enjoyment". Racked. Retrieved from https://www.racked.com/2018/6/15/17464614/goop-gwyneth-paltrow-skincare-supplements-transparency

Yurus, M. (2018, June 25). California considers creating a fake news advisory group. *CBS Sacramento*. Retrieved from https://sacramento.cbslocal.com/2018/06/25/california-considers-fake-news-advisory-group/

Zadrozny, B. (2019, June 14). Fake science led a mom to feed bleach to her autistic sons—and police did nothing to stop her. *NBC News*. Retrieved from https://www.nbcnews.com/tech/internet/fake-science-led-mom-fee-bleach-her-autistic-sons-police-n1017256

Zhang, J., Le, G., Larochelle, D., Pasick, R., Sawaya, G. F., Sarkar, U., & Centola, D. (2019). Facts or stories? How to use social media for cervical cancer prevention: a multi-method study of the effects of sender type and content type on increased message sharing. *Preventive Medicine*.

About the Author

David G. McAfee is a journalist and author of numerous books, including *No Sacred Cows* and *The Belief Book*. He holds a degree in English and Religious Studies from the University of California–Santa Barbara and lives in Southern California.